MIDLOTHIAN STATION WALKS

Brian Gould & Forbes Shepherd

DRUMLIN
WALKS

The authors have made every effort to ensure that the information provided in this publication is accurate and accept no responsibility whatsoever for any loss, injury or inconvenience experienced by any person or persons whilst using this book.

All maps from plotaroute.com with permission
All photographs of National Mining Museum Scotland with permission

The poem *Miners* on pages 20 and 21 is by *Wilfred Owen*.
*He wrote the poem shortly after leaving Craiglockhart Hospital,
Edinburgh where he had been treated for shell shock.*

The poem *The Gray Brother* on pages 88 and 89 is by *Sir Walter Scott*.
First published in the Minstrelsy of the Scottish Borders in 1803.

A catalogue record for this book is available from
the British Library. First published in 2023.

Copyright © Brian Gould and Forbes Shepherd, July 2023

All rights reserved. No part of this publication may be reproduced, stored in a retrieval system, or transmitted in any form or by any means, electronic or mechanical, including photocopying and recording, without prior permission in writing from the authors.

ISBN 978-1-3999-5983-4

Front cover photo: Borthwick Castle with the Pentland Hills in the distance

Printed by: ESC Packaging
Book design and development by: John Nicol
www.industrycottage.co.uk
Gorebridge, Scotland

ACKNOWLEDGEMENTS

This book was created with the support of others
and our thanks go to Archie Johnston, Bruce and Liz Brodie,
with a special thanks to John Nicol of Industry Cottage.

CONTENTS

Acknowledgments *5-6*
Introduction *8-9*
Useful Information *10-13*
History Of Midlothian *14-19*
Miners by Wilfred Owen *20-21*

SHAWFAIR SECTION	**22-33**

S1: Not Wasting Your Time 24-29
S2: Alien Terrain 30-33

ESKBANK SECTION	**36-87**

E1: Castle and Cliffs 38-49
E2: Maidens and Ice 50-55
E3: Ancient Bridges and Trees 56-59
E4: Sundials of Time 60-65
E5: The Gift of a Bridge 66-71
E6: A Kings Hunting Ground 74-81
E7: Water and Bridges 82-87
The Gray Brother by Sir Walter Scott *88-89*

NEWTONGRANGE SECTION　　　　　　　　　　　　　　90-113
N1: A Living Past 92-97
N2: Distant Views 100-105
N3: Up and Under 108-113

GOREBRIDGE SECTION　　　　　　　　　　　　　　114-163
G1: Moving Through Time 116-121
G2: An Explosive Past 122-127
G3: Bridges and Rivers 128-133
G4: Town of the Warriors 134-139
G5: Circle of Pitches 140-143
G6: A Witches Tale 146-151
G7: Castles and Churches 152-163

INTERSTATION WALKS　　　　　　　　　　　　　　166-183
IS1: Three Bridges 166-171
IS2: Birds of Prey 172-177
IS3: A Sloe Walk Through Time 178-183

Index *184-185*
About Drumlin Walks *186-187*

Midlothian Station Walks | 7

Looking towards the Pentland Hills from Masterton Wood

INTRODUCTION

Midlothian lies in the Scottish Lowlands and first emerged as a county in the Middle Ages and known as Edinburghshire until 1921. It covers an area of 353 sq. kms with the city of Edinburgh marking its northern boundary. To the west the Pentland Hills provide a clear physical frontier as do the Moorfoot Hills to the south and the Lammermuir Hills to the southeast. The highest point in Midlothian is Blackhope Scar (651m) on the border with Peebleshire.

The region has developed as an important commuter conurbation for **Edinburgh**, but agriculture remains a significant activity and sheep farming continues as it has done for generations in the surrounding hills.

The main towns are **Dalkeith, Bonnyrigg** and **Penicuik** and while there are no lochs of any significant size there are numerous large reservoirs mostly serving the city of **Edinburgh**. The landscape is marked by deep ravines and the glistening waters of the **Rivers North** and **South Esk** and **Gore Water**.

Its grand estates, houses and churches helped establish its early identity while coal and railways reshaped it again in the industrial age. The great buildings are strong reminders of the region's past and remnants of early industrial prosperity are everywhere to be seen. **Midlothian** has made its political mark and continues to act as a base for many writers and artists, while the great city of **Edinburgh** owes much to its southern neighbour.

USEFUL INFORMATION

This book describes 22 walks from the 4 Midlothian railway stations, Shawfair, Eskbank, Gorebridge and Newtongrange. There are 2 walks from Shawfair station; 7 from Eskbank; 7 from Gorebridge; 3 from Newtongrange and 3 interstation walks. Apart from the interstation walks all the routes return to the station where you started from.

Each walk has an information box giving its distance in km, approximate time to complete and the total ascent in metres. There is a brief description of the terrain and a difficulty rating based on one, two or three 'boots', one being the easiest. The time taken to complete each walk will vary according to fitness, weather conditions and your own desire to explore and linger!

Maps are provided with key points in the route numbered to correspond with the descriptor, and in some cases additional information is provided. Minor

obstacles are identified in some information boxes. Every care has been taken to ensure the descriptors and maps are as accurate as possible at the time of writing, but authors, publisher or landowners cannot be held responsible for any injury or accident, regardless of the cause.

The routes are varied: some are challenging and require boots and outdoor clothing, whereas others are more benign and can be walked without any specialist footwear or clothing.

OS Explorer Active 345 Lammermuir Hills: Dalkeith, Bonnyrigg & Gifford (2017) and OS Landranger (66) Edinburgh: Penicuik & North Berwick (2016) cover the areas of the walks.

Whatever the difficulty of the route, weather conditions will always need to be considered and you should be aware that in Scotland walking conditions can change very quickly. Most of the walks are low-level but some take you to higher ground where the weather can be more challenging.

USEFUL INFORMATION

There is also a need to be aware of the following:

Lambing: *March to May*

Cattle: *Take extra care when a field contains cattle, particularly if calves are also present. Keep to the field side and avoid completely if accompanied by a dog.*

Access Rights: *Within Scotland the 'right to roam' is enshrined in Law. The Land Reform (Scotland) Act 2003 established a legal right of access to most lands and waterways. A strong tradition of public access to the countryside has existed for centuries. While the law now supports this, a key emphasis within the Act is the onus on all involved to act responsibly. Several of the walks take you close to golf courses, through farms, across farmland and close to private properties. Please respect people's privacy and show consideration for the natural environment and for all those who make their living from it or make use of it for sport and recreation.*

The main points from the act are highlighted below and should be complied with.

Take responsibility for your own actions: *Care for your own safety, keep alert for hazards, and take special care with children.*

Respect people's privacy and peace of mind: *Do not act in ways that might annoy or alarm people, especially at night.*

Help land managers and others to work safely and effectively: *Keep clear of land management operations like harvesting or tree-felling, avoid damaging crops, and leave gates as you find them.*

Care for your environment: *Do not disturb wildlife and take your litter away with you.*

Keep your dog under proper control: *Dogs are popular companions but take special care if near livestock or during the bird breeding season, and always pick up after your dog.*

Access rights do not usually apply to farmyards but where a right of way or core path passes through one you have a right to proceed.

Local Annual Events
Dalkeith Local Festival: *First Saturday of August.*
Gorebridge Gala Day: *3rd Saturday in June*
Midlothian Outdoor Festival: *October*
Newtongrange Gala Day: *2nd Saturday in June*

Visitor Attractions
Dalkeith Country Park: *www.dalkeithcountrypark.co.uk*
Vogrie Country Park: *www.midlothian.gov.uk/info/200283/parks/236/vogrie_country_park/1*
Arniston House: *www.arnistonhouse.com*
National Mining Museum Scotland: *www.nationalminingmuseum.com*

A HISTORY OF MIDLOTHIAN

The history of Midlothian is dominated by its long association with religious belief; by the grand estates that occupy much of the landscape; by the part it played in driving industrial modernisation in Scotland and in the safe location it has provided for writers and artists.

One of its most striking features is a legacy of fine churches, castles and stately homes. The beauty and romance of 14th century **Rosslyn Chapel**, the famous religious site of **Newbattle Abbey**, the grandeur of **Dalkeith Palace** and other buildings all encapsulate the rich history of **Midlothian**.

Many of the large mansions date back to the 13th and 14th centuries, built as strongholds during the Anglo-Scots wars, with ownership staying with the same families for generations. Others have changed hands over the centuries with some falling into disrepair while others have

Crichton Castle

been damaged by fire and never restored.

Several great buildings have survived into the modern era and taken on different functions: **Newbattle Abbey** is now an adult education college, **Dalhousie** and **Borthwick Castles** are both high-end hotels while Midlothian Council have taken over responsibility for **Vogrie House**. These structures still exist in the landscape as reminders of the architectural and

A HISTORY OF MIDLOTHIAN

Newbattle Abbey

human history of **Midlothian**. Many of the churches in the area were built during the Victorian era as a 'mania for churches took told' designed to spread the gospel to both the urban and rural poor.

Rosslyn Chapel and **Newbattle Abbey** were built as Catholic institutions before the Reformation reorganised them into Protestant establishments. **Rosslyn Chapel** dates to the 15th century and was built by **William Sinclair 1st Earl of Caithness** and designed to celebrate Catholic ritual. Despite the claims made by the book, "The Da Vinci Code", any connection to the Knights Templar or the Holy Grail remain unproven! **Newbattle Abbey** was built by Cistercian monks in 1140 and was financially prosperous receiving major support from Scottish royalty. It derived much of its income from coal and the monks were known as the first Scottish coalminers.

The discovery of coal helped define the region. During the Carboniferous Period, around 300 million years ago, the **Midlothian** basin was warm with dense swampy forests which over time became compacted and turned into coal. Much later its exploitation as an energy source helped transform the area and led to the development of the Scottish economy. Coal-fuelled steam power led to further economic expansion allowing industrial production to take place in all weathers and locations.

By 1870 nearly 47,000 miners worked in 400 pits, most based in the rich coal fields of the Scottish central belt including **Midlothian.** Economic and political factors brought mining in the area to an end in the 1980s.

Monktonhall Colliery near **Danderhall** became the first privately owned mine in the UK when bought out by former workers in 1992. **Lady Victoria Colliery** in **Newtongrange** is now home to the **National Mining Museum** retaining many of its buildings and structures. It is considered the best-preserved example of a Victorian mine in Europe.

National Mining Museum

A HISTORY OF MIDLOTHIAN

Old railway parts at Birky Wood

The development of the railways greatly assisted the expansion of the coal industry. Their reliability as a transport system and the increase of the network in the 19th century were catalysts for huge social and economic change. **Midlothian** had at least five railway companies providing both passenger and freight services. As the road network expanded and the demands of industry changed all these railways disappeared in the late 1950s or early 1960s, victims of the Beeching cuts. There are many disused railway stations across the region, with the footprint of some remaining, while others, like the railways themselves, have disappeared into the landscape. Many larger structures still exist, among these is **Newbattle Viaduct** which opened in 1848 to carry the Waverley Route. With 23 arches running to a height of 26m, it returned to service with the opening of the **Borders Railway** in 2015.

The area has also played an important role in British culture and politics. In 1873 the Liberal politician **William Gladstone** conducted an election campaign designed to capture the local parliamentary seat. Such was his rhetorical skills and ability to engage the electorate that the so-called 'Midlothian campaign' was viewed as a turning point in British politics. During the campaign he addressed a crowd of 3000 from the balcony of the **Corn Exchange** in **Dalkeith**. In a series of long erudite speeches, he attacked the policies of then Prime Minister **Benjamin Disraeli**, undermining his government and setting the stage for **Gladstone's** return as a major political force and the Liberal's return to the national government.

The creator of romantic fiction, **Annie Shepherd Swan**, lived in **Gorebridge** and published over 200 books, serials and other works in the late 19th and early 20th century. She was politically active becoming a strong supporter of the suffragette cause before standing as a parliamentary candidate for a **Glasgow** constituency in 1922. She was also a founder member of the Scottish National Party.

William Drummond was a 17th century poet who lived at **Hawthornden Castle** above the **River North Esk**. His poetry was influenced by Italian and English masters and his style and tone are considered sensuous and beautiful with a dash of melancholy! The castle has been restored and now serves as a writers' retreat.

The great Scottish poet and novelist, **Sir Walter Scott**, also had a connection to the area and spent several summers from 1798 living in a cottage in **Lasswade,** where his literary career began.

The Borders Railway opened in 2015

MINERS

By Wilfred Owen
VERSE 1, 2 AND 7

There was a whispering in my hearth,
A sigh of the coal,
Grown wistful of a former earth
It might recall.

I listened for a tale of leaves
And smothered ferns,
Frond-forests, and the low sly lives
Before the fawns.

Comforted years will sit soft-chaired,
In rooms of amber,
The years will stretch their hands, well-cheered
By our life's ember;

SHAWFAIR

Shawfair

3rd Station from Waverley & 6th Station from Tweedbank

Shawfair is on the south-eastern edge of Edinburgh near Danderhall village and the hamlets of Millerhill and Newton Village. It is a new town in the making and when complete will have a town centre, 4000 homes, schools, retail outlets, business, leisure and community facilities comparable in size to Dalkeith and Linlithgow. There will also be a network of cycle and walking paths with landscaped green space.

The name of the site, Shawfair, comes from the nearby farm steading. The station opened in September 2015 as part of the Borders Railway designed to connect the new town to Edinburgh.

There is a history of coal mining with Scotland's last superpit, Monktonhall Colliery once dominating the area. It was sunk in the 1950s to supply the new generation of power stations and started producing coal in 1967, replacing the nearby Woolmet Colliery.

At one time Woolmet's huge bing was a prominent landmark on Edinburgh's skyline until it was levelled and landscaped in the late 1980s /early 1990s by the former Lothian Regional Council.

The miners' memorial garden in Danderhall contains plaques to those who lost their lives in accidents at Monktonhall and Woolmet Collieries. It also commemorates the children who worked down mines before the abolition of child labour.

Energy production now comes in the form of biogas from food waste at the Kelda Organic Energy Plant and heat from waste at Millerhill Recycling and Energy Recovery Centre.

During WW11 a decoy anti-aircraft battery site was built near Shawfair Farm to deceive enemy bombers and reconnaissance aircraft by using techniques from stage and screen. The derelict site with its four emplacements and command post can still be seen today.

Please be aware that over the next few years, local developments may impact walking routes in the area.

SHAWFAIR: *WALK 1*

S1 A CHANGING LANDSCAPE

Industrial waste has been reformed and landscaped into a public space for all to enjoy. There are splendid views to the Pentland Hills, the Firth of Forth and across to Fife while a reminder of the ingenuity required during the last war is still in place.

1. Leave Shawfair Station car park, turn left and follow the pavement as it passes over the railway to the main road. Cross with care to the short stretch of road directly ahead and past a few houses to join the narrow path at a metal barrier. Within a few metres, as the path divides, keep left and follow the track along the edge of a field.

SHAWFAIR: *WALK 1*

2. Just before reaching the road turn right into a large field and join the path that runs between a fence line and a deep ditch. (To visit a miners' memorial garden, do not turn right but keep ahead on the pavement – to site at Danderhall)

There is a short ascent that takes you past a football pitch and when the fence line ends keep right up the slope to a line of bushes. As they end turn sharply right and follow a wide path as it traverses the hill to a plinth that once held a mining memorial. Turn left onto the wide grass track to the top of the bing and as you do so a dramatic panorama opens up. To the south you see the Border Hills, looking out west the ancient volcano that is Arthur's Seat sits above Edinburgh and north beyond the Firth of Forth is the Kingdom of Fife. Kestrels and buzzards are common here as they hover above looking for prey.

Miners' Memorial Garden
The miners' memorial garden in Danderhall is dedicated to the miners that lost their lives at Monktonhall and Woolmet Collieries. It also commemorates the children who worked down the mines until the abolition of child labour in 1933.

Buzzards and Kestrels
The buzzard is the most common of Britain's larger birds of prey. Its mewing 'kiew' is a familiar sound as it soars effortlessly on rising thermals.

The kestrel's most distinctive characteristic is its ability to hover using its fanned tail to keep it stabilised as it hunts for its prey. Buzzards can also hover but not quite so gracefully.

SHAWFAIR: **WALK 1**

Woolmet Colliery
Woolmet Colliery opened in 1904 with over 800 people working the mine. 305m (1000 feet) below the surface the pit produced more than 200,000 tonnes of coal a year. It operated until 1966 when it was replaced by the more modern Monktonhall Colliery.

At one time Woolmet's huge bing was a prominent landmark on Edinburgh's skyline until it was levelled and landscaped. The name Woolmet means 'hermit's retreat' or the 'place of the cave'. From the top of the bing look for a path that drops right towards the road below. On reaching it turn left and when a metal barrier appears (look out for an old, wooded sign indicating when the land was reclaimed) on your right head through and cross the road with care before turning left.

3. Turn right onto a single-track road and past some large houses. As you leave them behind the road rises to provide views towards the Firth of Forth and Fife. On your left under the pylons are the derelict remains of a WWII decoy site which is well worth a visit.

4. On meeting a row of cottages, turn right past farm buildings before joining the track that drops downhill between fields to arrive close to the railway. Keep ahead past a pond and follow the track towards the road, cross, turn left and return to the station.

WWII Decoy Site
The decoy anti-aircraft battery site or "starfish" site is now derelict, but the command post and four emplacements are still standing. It was constructed during WWII to deceive enemy bombers and reconnaissance aircraft bound for Edinburgh by using techniques from the stage and screen.

SHAWFAIR: *WALK 2*

S2 ALIEN TERRAIN

Enter a strange landscape of shattered stone and scattered vegetation, the remnants of mining producing an alien terrain atop this man-made spoil heap.

1. Head away from the station on the entrance road, turn left and continue ahead to cross the road bridge over the railway. As the pavement dips down cross to join a roadway which goes towards a large yard before heading over an earth barrier.

Continue past a small pond which contains stands of reeds and bull rushes acting as a haven

SHAWFAIR: *WALK 1*

Graffiti
Graffiti has a long history and has been found in ancient Roman ruins and Medieval English Churches and is a form of visual communication while also an expressive art form. It is the marking of a public space by an individual or a group and is usually illegal.

for wildlife including swans, coots, moorhen and tufted ducks. Foxgloves and orchids can be s een here in the spring.

Keep right beyond the pond and follow the fence line up the slope. You pass an unused bridge with some impressive graffiti, beyond is a food treatment plant

Bing
A bing is the Scottish term for spoil heaps created from the waste produced by mining. They can be seen throughout Scotland with many transformed into open public spaces where wildlife flourish.

dominating the opposite bank. Head up a short steep rutted section to arrive on Shawfair bing. Follow a clear track ahead across this man-made spoil heap. The track swings left to join an embankment with fine views of the Pentland Hills.

2. When the path descends to a flat area, turn left, then quickly right towards the far bank. Proceed up the slope to follow a path that runs close to the edge of the bing across an area of shattered stone and isolated stands of buddleia and silver birch.

On reaching the corner of the bing head right through bushes down a short steep slope close to a large farm shed. Head past on an area of open ground towards a farm track next to a wall in front of you.

3. Turn left and descend between fields to the pond you passed earlier. Head out to the road before crossing, turning left and returning to the station.

Harvest time in Midlothian

ESKBANK

Newbattle Abbey

4th Station from Waverley & 5th Station from Tweedbank

Dalkeith existed as far back as 1142 when it was mentioned in the Charter of the Abbey of Holyrood, and grew from the 12th century castle on the site of Dalkeith Palace. Eskbank is considered to be the most affluent part of the town containing many fine large Victorian houses. The first of these was built in Glenesk Terrace in 1794 for Thomas Brown the minister of Newbattle Parish Church. When the railway station opened in 1849 many Edinburgh merchants and professionals built houses locally.

Eskbank Station sits eight miles south of Edinburgh with the original station being closed in 1969 as part of the Beeching cuts. The current station lies further south of the original and was opened in 2015 as part of the Borders Railway. It sits within a commercial area with many large stores and outlets accessible from the footbridge that crosses the railway.

Dalkeith Solar Meadow, opened in 2013, occupies a 5 acre site close to the station where it produces over 500,000 kilowatt hours of electricity annually and serves as an outdoor classroom for engineering students. Opposite the Solar Meadow is the Midlothian Campus of Edinburgh College, which has a total of four campuses around the city.

Montagu Bridge, a wedding gift for Lady Elizabeth Montagu, can be found in Dalkeith Country Park. Close by is a twelve-sided conservatory, now glassless, that was used for growing oranges and figs. There is a veteran oak wood, a designated Site of Special Scientific Interest, where some of the trees are over 900 years old and where kings once hunted.

St Nicholas Buccleuch Church in Dalkeith hosted Cromwell's troops and provided stables for the horses during his occupation of Southern Scotland. The notorious witchfinder Reverend Calderwood was a parish minister whose efforts led to a large increase in those accused and tried of witchcraft.

ESKBANK: WALK 1

E1 CASTLES & CLIFFS

This long route takes you on a journey through history, from a dismantled railway to a ruined gunpowder works. In Roslin Glen, a castle, magnificent ancient woodland and spectacular cliffs are all encountered.

1. Cross the footbridge at Eskbank Station and follow the path as it loops left to an industrial estate. When the path ends turn right and within a few metres keep left at the finger post for Bonnyrigg. This is the Musselburgh to Penicuik Cycle Walkway which follows the route of the old railway. Follow

ESKBANK: *WALK 1*

Roslin Gunpowder Mills
Roslin Gunpowder Mill was once the largest gunpowder factory in Scotland which opened for production in 1801 and was in operation for over 150 years. Gunpowder was used in the mining industry and for munitions from the time of the Napoleonic Wars until the Second World War. It was exported from Edinburgh's ports all over the world. Charcoal, made from local wood, was combined with sulphur and saltpetre from India to make the gunpowder. The mill was originally powered by water taken from the nearby River North Esk to the mill's waterwheel.

this sign-posted path across the footbridge over the A7 and through housing to the side of Cockpen Road. Take the crossing through the ornate barrier and past the remains of the platform that was once Bonnyrigg Station which closed to passengers in 1962. Continue through housing for another km to reach farmland where the path then runs parallel to the main road.

2. Just before the roundabout cross to a roadway opposite. Cross and head into the grounds of grounds of Roslin Glen Country Park. Continue through farmland on what was once the track bed of the Penicuik railway with good views of the Pentland Hills. After passing under a bridge, you arrive at the old Rosslyn Castle Station platform, its name set into the bank in small white stones. It was opened in 1872 by the Penicuik Railway and closed to passengers in 1951 but remained open to freight until 1967. Past the bridge is a picnic area, once the goods yard which had a dedicated siding for the Gunpowder works.

3. Not far from the station, next to an information board and the sign for Roslin Country Park, turn right up the steps and then down the slope into the grounds of what was once Roslin Gunpowder Mills, which operated for over 150 years. As you get to the River North Esk, there is a weir and a mill lade

Rosslyn Castle
Rosslyn Castle was built in the early 14th century on a promontory surrounded by the River North Esk on three sides. Additions and repairs were made to the castle over the next three centuries due to frequent mishaps, including a fire in 1447. Cromwell's troops attacked the castle in 1651 using canons situated on higher ground. A house built out of the castle's remains is now a holiday let. The castle is also featured in Sir Walter Scott's poem 'Rosabelle'. Legend tells us that it is home to a sleeping lady who, when awake, will show the location of treasure buried deep within its vaults.

Midlothian Station Walks | 41

ESKBANK: *WALK 1*

Roslin Glen

Roslin Glen is the largest and most diverse surviving example of ancient woodland in Midlothian and is a Site of Special Scientific Interest (SSSI). Here the River North Esk flows through a 1.5km long gorge with sheer cliffs up to a height of 30m of pinkish red Roslin sandstone. At one time the

river was very polluted due to the industries that have long gone. The river is now home to dippers and kingfishers with otters making their home along the riverbank.

which diverted water to power a waterwheel that in turn powered the Roslin Gunpowder Mills.

On crossing the bridge take the steps down to the ruined buildings that once housed the waterwheel. Note the impressive sandstone cliffs on the other side of the river.

Take your time to explore this magical place where some scenes of the Reckoning from the Outlander TV series were filmed. Follow the path that runs close to the river, up some wooden steps and past another mill building before joining the main track. Further on, pass some ruined buildings set into the hillside, designed to contain any explosions to avoid setting off a chain reaction that could destroy the rest of the buildings. The track leads you out through the old mill entrance to the main road.

4. Cross the sharp and dangerous bend with care and head downhill. Beyond the bridge turn

ESKBANK: *WALK 1*

left to join the path adjacent to the wastewater treatment plant before climbing steep steps to the roadside. Turn right next to the safety barrier and when the pavement ends, right again onto the track that runs alongside a large field. You pass through an area thick with horsetail which is a type of fern that reproduces by spores rather than seeds. Its stems are covered with an abrasive silicone making it useful as a pot scrubber!

As the path rises, with a cemetery on either side, you arrive at a small road junction. Continue ahead a short distance to visit Rosslyn Chapel. Otherwise, turn right and before you is the dramatic elevated entrance to what is left of the 14th century Rosslyn Castle which is well worth a visit. Before the main gate take the steps on the right to the base of the castle and head under the magnificent sandstone archway. The remains of an old bridge support that once provided access to the castle over the river are ahead of you.

5. Bear left on the clear path as it winds its way through woodland with the deep gorge of Roslin Glen below. Follow the path uphill where the remains of General Moncks Battery can be seen consisting of a ditch below raised ground. This was where Cromwell's troops located their cannons to attack Rosslyn Castle in 1651. At the top of the rise, pass under a row of yew trees on top of a low stone terrace bordering Rosebank House. The path continues through this ancient semi-natural habitat of mixed deciduous woodland, made up mostly of ash, oak, and elm. Roslin Glen is a Special Site of Scientific Interest (SSSI) containing over 200 species of flowering plants.

As the path levels look to your right through the trees for the magnificent 17th century Hawthorden Castle which is perched high on the sandstone cliffs overlooking the deep gorge of the river. Just beyond the path turns left out of the woodland to run across an area of wet ground

Hewnan Bank

Hewnan Bank is an SSSI due to its geology as a rare exposure of Midland Valley glacial deposits. The Midland Valley lay between the Highland boundary fault and the Southern Upland fault. Some of the oldest rocks in the Midland Valley date back 470 million years. They consist of 2 different till layers that were deposited when the Scottish Ice Sheet receded at the end of the last Ice Age. The area is prone to landslides and is home to a colony of sand martins.

ESKBANK: *WALK 1*

The path near the old Rosslyn Castle Station platform

Baird Smith Memorial
The Baird Smith Memorial is a large and imposing monument with its wealth of decorative carving and bronze plaques giving it a grand appearance. It commemorates two important local figures. Dr Richard Smith was a surgeon in the Royal Navy and moved to Lasswade in 1818 to take up private practice. His eldest son Richard Baird Smith was born in 1818 and raised in Lasswade and was an engineer with the British army in India.

to a series of raised planks. A short incline takes you alongside a large field. When the fence ends, take a sharp right down a steep slope to an exposed area where Scots Pine cling to the edge of the gorge with sheer drops to the river below. Keep to the path above this until you reach a bend in the river with a series of information boards.

6. Take the steps left up the side of the field. Alternatively take a diversion to visit Maiden Castle. This is not actually a castle, but a fort defined by a single earthen rampart and inner ditch, which together enclose an elongated oval area. On leaving keep to the higher path which will rejoin the track up from the river but take care as it is narrow in places.

Either path option goes to a fingerpost directing you to Polton. Continue left up more steps to the top of this bank and head across this flat area to the gateway. Turn right to Polton and descend to Hewnan Bank which is an SSSI.

Cross this exposed banking with care as it drops precipitously on both sides and continue on the path as it descends the bank on steps guarded by a handrail. Turn left and leave the woodland onto the public road close to Polton.

7. Turn right onto a sharp dangerous bend that must be negotiated with care and before the bridge, turn left onto the roadway leading to housing. At a house entrance keep right onto

Hawthornden Castle

Hawthornden Castle is a 15th century ruin with a 17th century house sitting on cliffs overlooking the deep gorge on the River North Esk, originally owned by the poet William Drummond. The castle is now a writer's retreat, patronised by authors such as Ian Rankin, and is owned by the philanthropist Drue Heinz, the publisher of the Paris Review and widow of H.J. Heinz. Below the castle are man-made caves that have been in existence much longer than the castle itself.

ESKBANK: *WALK 1*

the path that runs alongside the River North Esk towards Mavisbank and Lasswade. Continue along the riverbank then bear left into the large field in which there is a prominent modern house on the banking with a doocot off to its left. A doocot, also called a dovecot, is used to house pigeons. Leave the field on the right through the gate and follow the path up the slope on concrete steps between garden walls.

On reaching the top, cross directly to the path that takes you right above two single-track roads. On meeting the road, turn right past the entrance gate of a large house before re-joining the path, after which the village of Lasswade and viaduct come into view. On meeting the road, head uphill and through a large gateway just beyond the Lasswade Old Kirk Cemetery entrance. Very quickly you encounter the large and imposing Baird Smith Memorial which commemorates two local figures. The more prominent of those was Dr Richard Smith, a highly respected local doctor who would visit patients in all weathers, riding his shaggy brown pony, Paddy. Keep right and take the narrow 'Coffin Lane' as it drops to the main road.

8. Turn right to the pedestrian crossing and keep left on the far side and keep right to cross the river on the footbridge. Stay right, then left, to follow the main road uphill. Once it levels out past Pittendreich Care Centre, there is a fingerpost for Dalkeith Penicuik Walkway. Cross this very fast road with care and follow the wide track that runs through Broomieknowe Golf Course and downhill close to houses on the main road. Take the crossing and follow a wide grass strip with houses on the right and up a set of steps, turn left and follow the signs back to the station.

Roslin Gunpowder Mill

Rosslyn Chapel (Formerly St Mathews Collegiate Church)
Rosslyn Chapel was built in the 15th century as a chapel for the St Clair family who own it to this day. During the reformation, the chapel fell into disrepair and in 1650 Cromwell's troops stabled their horses there. During the Victorian era the chapel was repaired and in 1862 weekly services began. In 1914 a suffragette bomb exploded inside the church. The Chapel came to worldwide notice through The DaVinci Code, a novel by Dan Brown, also featured in a film of the same name.

ESKBANK: *WALK 2*

E2 — MAIDENS & ICE

Follow in the footsteps of monks and royalty crossing the narrow Maiden Bridge named after Henry VII's daughter, Margaret, as she made her way to marry King James IV in 1503. Marvel also at the 17th century grotto that hides the entrance to an old icehouse.

1. Leave the station past Edinburgh College and Dalkeith Solar Meadow, Scotland's first solar farm. On meeting the main road turn right and within a few hundred metres cross to enter woodland through an opening in the wall with a fingerpost for Eskbank. Turn right and follow the path as it drops through

ESKBANK: *WALK 2*

trees to the side of a burn with a housing estate beyond. Follow the fence line, cross the road, and continue to the trees in front of you.

2. Head into the woodland and on reaching the metal railing turn left and follow the path along the tree-lined River South Esk.

As you pull away from the river there is an impressive Redwood tree which can grow to over 300 feet and live for 2000 years or more. On arriving at the rear of housing follow the roadway to meet Newbattle Road.

3. Cross the road with care, turn right then left onto the roadway

Icehouse
The 17th century grotto hides the entrance to the icehouse which has a brick-built egg-shaped pit, 12 ft in diameter which would have been filled with ice in winter to store meat and other perishables. An iron bridge once led to the grotto but has been replaced with a new wooden structure.

Maiden Bridge
Maiden Bridge was renamed after Henry VII's daughter, Margaret Tudor. In 1503, on her way to marry King James IV, she stopped at Newbattle Abbey to be blessed by the monks. She was accompanied by the Earl of Surrey at the head of 500 men-at-arms and stopped at Newbattle Abbey before meeting her future spouse. This marriage paved the way for the Union of the Crowns a hundred years later.

ESKBANK: WALK 2

that drops to the old Newbattle Bridge, parts of which date back to the 16th century. Unusually, the refuge area for pedestrians crossing the bridge is pointed on one side and semi-circular on the other.

4. On crossing the bridge enter woodland at the sign for Lord Ancrum's Wood and past a monkey puzzle tree. This diverse woodland contains native and non-native species dating back over 200 years. On meeting a path junction keep left to the riverside and through woodland as it edges this beautiful section of the River South Esk. You pass a 17th century icehouse which was used to store meat and perishables, opposite sits the impressive Newbattle Abbey College. Continue along the river where dippers can be seen and if lucky, the colourful flash of a kingfisher looking for a meal.

5. At Maiden Bridge cross the 15th century structure over the River South Esk. Built for monks at nearby Newbattle Abbey it helped link it to Soutra Aisle, once Scotland's most important medieval hospital. Keep ahead to where a fingerpost for Eskbank directs you left through woodland to the edge of a housing estate.

Newbattle Abbey

6. Head through the barrier to the pavement opposite. The high wall was once part of the Newbattle Abbey grounds and at one time housed St David's High School before it was demolished and replaced with housing. At the junction with the main road keep left and within a few metres cross with care this busy road to an opening next to Newbattle Cemetery.

7. Follow the path up the slope through woodland, carpeted with wild garlic in spring which can be foraged and used in salads or made into pesto. The path levels out to the gateway where you first entered the woodland. Cross the road with care and turn left to meet the sign for Eskbank Station that directs you alongside cottages. Follow the path as this crosses the railway and take an immediate right onto a grass path. Where this ends pass through the gate before turning right across the railway to the station.

Wild Garlic
From March onwards wild garlic is easily identified by its white starry flowers giving rise to a dazzling white carpet. On warm days its distinctive smell hangs in the air. It is also an ancient woodland plant indicator and has been traditionally used as a remedy for rheumatism and high cholesterol.

ESKBANK: *WALK 3*

E3 — ANCIENT BRIDGES & TREES

Reminders of different times are ever present as historic bridges and ancient woodlands evoke images of royal grandeur and the rural legacy left by our forbearers.

1. Leave the station and head past Edinburgh College and Dalkeith Solar Meadow, which generates 0.6MW of electricity annually, to the main road. Turn right and after a short distance cross into woodland through a large wall opening with a fingerpost for Eskbank. Keep directly ahead through the trees to emerge at the roadside next to Newbattle Cemetery which has been in use for over 200 years. Cross with care, keeping left on the pavement to the roundabout before bearing right alongside

ESKBANK: WALK 3

Lord Ancrum
Michael Ancrum was the 13th Marquess of Lothian and a prominent Conservative politician in the 1980s and 1990s. He served under two Prime ministers, John Major and Margaret Thatcher and occupied numerous government roles during his career. In 2010 he entered the House of Lords taking the title, Baron Kerr of Monteviot.

the high wall that was once part of the Newbattle Abbey grounds.

2. As the road swings right, cross to the opening in the far corner and go through the metal barrier into trees. At the fingerpost turn right to the narrow medieval Maiden Bridge. It was crossed by Henry VII's daughter, Margaret, on her way to marry King James IV in 1503. Accompanied by the Earl of Surrey at the head of 500 men-at-arms, she stopped at Newbattle Abbey to obtain a blessing from the monks before meeting her future spouse. Beyond the bridge, head up the roadway to your right towards Newbattle Golf Course.

3. As the track swings right keep ahead to cross an earth barrier. Within less than a 100m of this turn right to join a path through woodland with the golf course on your right. Continue on this winding path for a km to arrive at a wide woodland track. Turn left and within a few metres, turn right and continue to where a water drain cuts across the track. Just beyond, turn right onto a path close to the stream that runs from the drain. This is Lord Ancrum's Wood whose name comes from the title held by the Kerr family, former owners of the wood and later donated by them to the Scottish nation.

4. Follow the path as it winds its way downhill through this diverse woodland which contains native and non-native species dating back over 200 years. It includes ash, oak, beech, chestnut, Douglas fir and yew with many of the older trees producing an abundance of bracket fungus. On meeting a T- junction, turn left up the slope and follow the path to the roadside.

5. Turn right and cross Old Newbattle Bridge, built in the 16th century and rebuilt later by the Victorians. From here you can see the new bridge erected in 1956. Head to the main road after passing close to an impressive row of cottages lined with cypress trees.

6. Cross the road with care and within 50m, turn left onto the narrow roadway past housing into woodland. Where the path meets the banks of the River South Esk keep right alongside the river, crossing the banking of an old road before arriving next to a railing protecting a storm drain.

7. Turn right here onto the grassland that runs between housing before crossing the road to the bank of trees before you. Find the path in the corner close to a burn and head up the bank into the woodland. Within 500m you return to the original opening in the wall, cross the road with care and retrace your route back to the station.

Bracket Fungus
Bracket fungi, or shelf fungi, play an important role in nutrient recycling and carbon dioxide production within woodlands. Known as polyphores they are much more common in older woodlands and over 1000 species have been identified. While they can damage trees, they are also used in traditional medicines to make herbal tea. Deforestation has threatened the existence of some species.

ESKBANK: *WALK 4*

E4 MINING MONKS

Follow in the steps of Scotland's first coal miners to where a monastery was founded as far back as 1140. Admire the formal gardens with their 17th century sundials set within this tranquil area.

1. Take the footbridge from the station over the railway and immediately turn left through a gate onto a grass path. On meeting a bridge, cross and continue past cottages to the main road. Keep left and cross the road with care when you see an old gateway set in the wall opposite with a fingerpost for Eskbank. Continue under a high canopy of trees to the side of the public road next to Newbattle Cemetery.

ESKBANK: *WALK 4*

Newbattle Abbey
Newbattle Abbey stands on the site of a monastery founded in 1140 by Cistercian monks from Melrose Abbey to which Newbattle was affiliated. The Abbey soon became prosperous, the main source of income coming from the coal mines. The monks were among the first, if not the first, coal miners in Scotland and traces of these early mines can still be found in the grounds of the Abbey. During the Scottish wars with England, it was burned or sacked on several occasions.

Newbattle Abbey College
The Abbey became a private residence in 1587 and remained so until 1937 when Philip Kerr, 11th Marquess of Lothian gifted the house to the nation for use as a further education college. It is known as Newbattle Abbey College and offers a mixture of Arts and Social Sciences courses along with Rural Skills for adults.
It is said to be haunted by a Grey Lady who is the spirit of a girl who was killed because she fell in love with one of the monks.

In the gardens of Newbattle Abbey

2. Cross with care and follow the pavement left towards the roundabout then right into Newbattle Gardens passing an impressive high wall that was once part of the grounds of Newbattle Abbey. As the road turns right, cross and head into woodland known as Benbught Wood. Follow the path as it winds through yew trees to emerge at a single-track road. Turn right and before reaching Maiden Bridge, turn right on the track into woodland and towards the riverbank.

3. Follow this path, lined with beech trees, into the grounds of Newbattle Abbey College which stands in the grounds of a monastery founded in 1140 Close to the main building, on the right is a formal garden which was laid out in the mid-19th century. There are two sundials dating from 1635 that used to adorn the front of the house, both of which are well worth a visit.

ESKBANK: *WALK 4*

North and South Sundials
The North and South sundials were made in 1635 and originally adorned the front of Newbattle Abbey House. They were moved to the gardens at the rear of the house where they stand on plinths made in the 19th century.

The entrance to Newbattle Abbey

4. Leave the grounds of the College along the main drive to the entrance and cross the road before turning left over the River South Esk. Beyond the bridge take the opening in the wall into the woodland to a set of steps. At the top, keep right and follow the path through this mixed woodland. Pass with care a section with a precarious drop on the right.

5. At the side of the main road turn right past the Sun Inn with the impressive Newbattle Viaduct before you. The arches are lined with three layers of brick, and most are reinforced with iron strapping, as are the bridge piers. As the pavement ends take a right through a clear opening onto the path that runs next to a large field and past the rear of housing.

6. On reaching a large grass expanse between houses turn left to the roadside. Cross, pass under some trees and keep ahead to where a small burn runs alongside the path. Head up the slope to the wall opening where you first entered the woodland. Cross the road with care, turn right, and return to the station.

Sun Inn
The Sun Inn lies close to the River South Esk on 5 acres of wooded ground. It is an old coaching inn and was the first staging post for stagecoaches travelling from Edinburgh to London. It is now a pub that serves delicious food and AA Four Star boutique hotel.

ESKBANK: *WALK 5*

E5 — THE GIFT OF A BRIDGE

Cross the extravagant wedding gift of a bridge to Lady Elizabeth Montagu, once adorned with three life-sized stag sculptures. It spans the River North Esk in this 1000 acre estate.

1. At the top of the station platform ramp continue ahead on the tree-lined footpath, past the rear of Edinburgh College to the pedestrian crossing. Cross and turn left before turning down Ancrum Road, the third opening on your right. On meeting the main road, cross and turn left before taking the first opening on your right down Park Road.

2. At the end of the road enter Kings Park and follow the path through the park to the main road. Turn right, cross the road at the crossing opposite Morrisons supermarket and continue right into the centre of Dalkeith, with its mixture of old and new

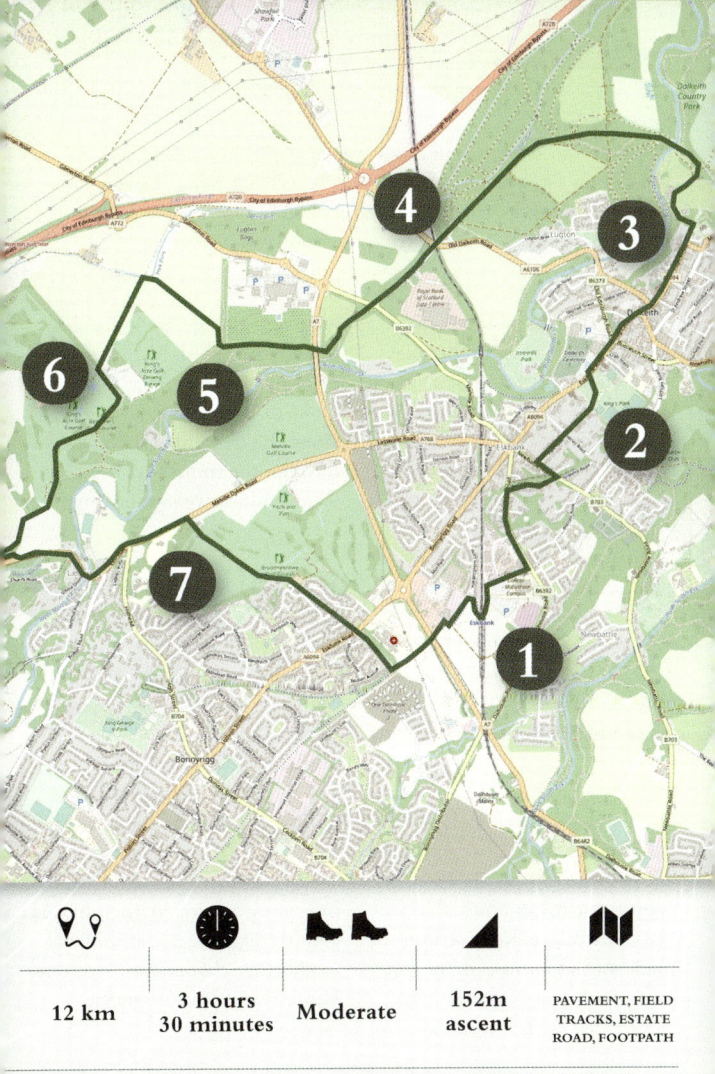

ESKBANK: *WALK 5*

Corn Exchange
The Corn Exchange, once the largest grain market in Scotland, built in 1854 in the Jacobean architectural style. In 1904, a young Winston Churchill attended a political meeting there. It is now home to Melville Housing Association and a museum managed by the Dalkeith Historical Society.

buildings. Beyond the main shopping centre is St Nicholas Buccleuch Parish Church which was used as temporary lodgings and stables for Cromwell's troops in 1650. Further along the High Street on your right, set back from the road, is the Corn Exchange where both Gladstone and Churchill have spoken.

3. Continue to the entrance gates to Dalkeith Country Park, which covers an area of 1000 acres and is owned by the Buccleuch Living Heritage Trust. On your right, sits St Mary's Episcopal Church, built in 1843 as a chapel for Dalkeith Palace. Take the roadway to your left past the impressive 18th century mansion house that is Dalkeith Palace. Keep left on the roadway to the main drive and cross the River North Esk on Montagu Bridge, built as a gift to Lady Elizabeth Montagu to celebrate her marriage to the 3rd Duke of Buccleuch. Continue along the tree-lined driveway through the impressive King's Gate, built to welcome King George IV in 1882.

4. Keep left and take the crossing to the other side and head right then left and continue to the roundabout. Cross this junction with care and head into the grounds of Melville Castle Hotel which sits in 54 acres of estate and was a favourite destination of Mary, Queen of Scots. As the road begins to drop, you meet a rough parking area with a sign indicating a bridle path. Join this path through trees and under a road bridge that is home to some impressive colourful graffiti.

5. As the path begins to rise turn right on a tree-lined path that runs between fields to a derelict building. Turn left past it to join a wide strip of land. There are views towards the Pentland Hills which run for 30 km west of Edinburgh. The path passes an old wooden rail wagon to an intersection before turning left on a farm track towards Kings Acre Golf Course.

6. Enter through a large metal gate and take an immediate left to join the main entrance road to the golf course. The clubhouse welcomes walkers and refreshments are available to take away. This a good opportunity to take a well-earned rest and look out over this beautiful 18-hole golf course which occupies a 135 acre site which was formerly a working dairy farm.

Follow the long driveway through the golf course to the main road and downhill to Lasswade. On meeting Luci's Restaurant and Cocktail Bar, turn left and take the footbridge

St. Nicholas Buccleuch Parish Church

This ancient church was built in 1420 and enlarged in 1475, although an earlier chapel on this site may date back to the 11th century. The church was used as accommodation for men and horses when Cromwell invaded Scotland in 1650. Between 1851 and 1854 the church was rebuilt with a new steeple, which was in turn replaced, after a fire in 1885. The 'cutty' stool where sinners were forced to sit and repent was also lost in the fire.

ESKBANK: WALK 5

Dalkeith Palace
The present palace was built in 1711 on the site of the 12th century Dalkeith Castle. It is currently owned by the Buccleuch Living Heritage Trust. Bonnie Prince Charlie stayed here during the 1745 Jacobite Rebellion and Queen Victoria visited in 1842. The palace is said to be haunted by the spirit of a young girl who fell from an upstairs window.

over the River North Esk. At the war memorial, take the steps and right onto the road then turn left past houses, before joining the pavement on the busy main road and head uphill. The name Lasswade is derived from the Gaelic Leas Bhaid which means 'the clump at the fort.'

7. Just past Pittendreich Care Centre there is a fingerpost for the Dalkeith Penicuik Walkway, cross and follow the wide track through Broomieknowe Golf Course. Continue on this track as it drops between houses. When meeting the main road, take the crossing to the grassy area that runs between a strip of trees and the back of housing. Take the steps at the end and turn left onto the Penicuik to Dalkeith Cycle Walkway, which follows the route of the old railway that closed in 1967. Follow the footpath over the main road to an industrial area, keep right, then left onto the footpath that returns you to the station.

Bluebells in the forest

Melville Castle Hotel
Melville Castle estate dates to 1125 but the design of the current building has remained unchanged since 1786. Mary, Queen of Scots was a frequent visitor here, as was Sir Walter Scott who mentions the estate in his poem The Gray Brother. The castle was unoccupied and fell into a state of disrepair in the 1980s but was purchased by the Hays Trust in 1993 and extensively renovated. It is now a luxury hotel, brasserie and events venue.

Montagu Bridge
Montagu Bridge spans the River North Esk and is the work of the great architect, Robert Adam. It was a gift for Lady Elizabeth Montagu to celebrate her marriage to the 3rd Duke of Buccleuch. There were three life-sized sculptures of stags on the bridge parapet, but they were removed as they frightened the horses.

The gates to Dalkeith Country Park

ESKBANK: WALK 6

E6 — A KINGS HUNTING GROUND

Walk back through time under a magnificent ancient oak forest with some trees over 900 years old. Imagine Kings of Old riding on their mighty steeds between the majestic oaks hunting for deer.

1. Leave the station through the car park and on meeting the main road turn right. After a few hundred metres cross and enter woodland through a wide opening in the wall, signposted for Eskbank. Keep ahead and follow the path through trees and past Newbattle Cemetery where the first internment was in 1813 and they continue to this day.

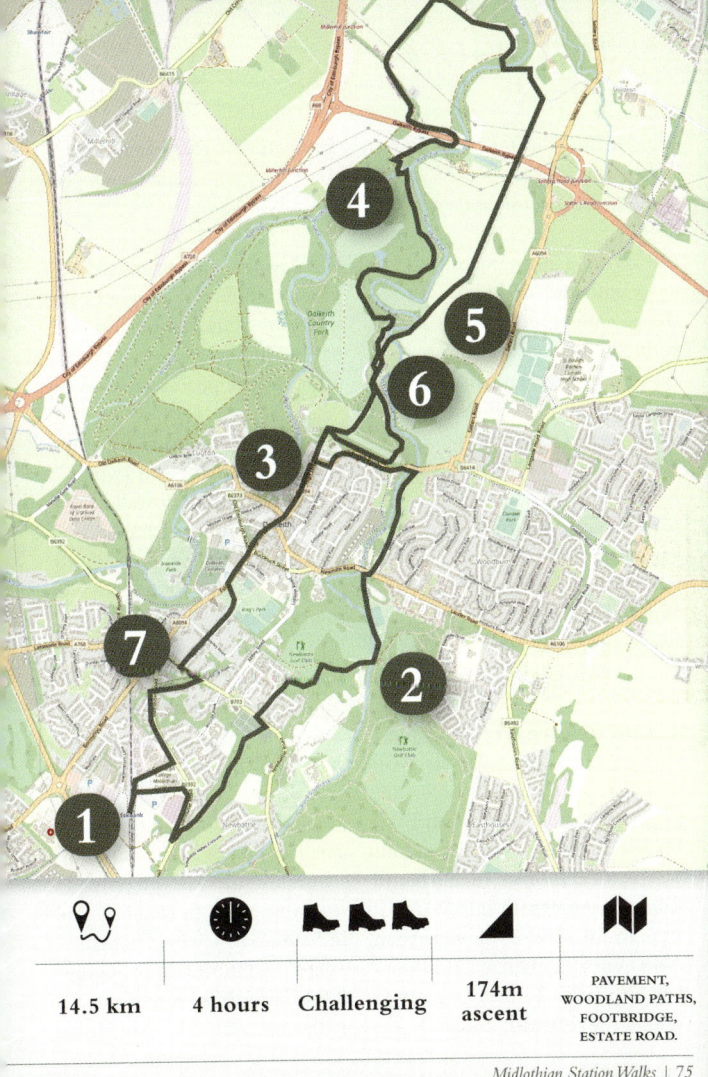

ESKBANK: WALK 6

Salters Road
Maiden Bridge was the ancient crossing point over the River South Esk for Salters Road. This was used by the monks to transport coal to Prestonpans and salt and seafood on the return journey to Newbattle.

On arriving at the roadside cross with care and follow the pavement left towards the roundabout then right into Newbattle Gardens passing an impressive high wall that was once part of the grounds of Newbattle Abbey. Where the road turns right, cross at the parking area and go through the gap in the fence into an area of woodland, known as Benbught Wood. Follow the path as it winds through yew trees to emerge at a single-track road.

2. Turn right and cross Maiden Bridge, a narrow medieval structure which was the crossing point over the River South Esk for the ancient Salters Road built by the local monks. Turn left and follow the footpath into Waterfall Park to the side of the main road. Cross with care, turn right then left into James Lean Avenue to where the footpath descends left through a large, grassed area. Close to the road turn left over the footbridge and stay on the pavement past a safety barrier and uphill to the pedestrian crossing.

Cross, turn left and follow the narrow pavement as it swings along the boundary wall of Dalkeith Country Park to the cobbled entrance roadway into the estate. The park has been in the Buccleuch family for over 300 years and the site itself can be traced all the way back to Roman times. The palace and the park were used during both world wars by British and Polish troops.

3. Continue through the formal gateway past St Mary's Episcopal Church which has the only working water-powered organ in Scotland. Stay on the main estate road until you reach the Restoration Yard, a renovated 18th century stables containing

Wooden bridge over the River North Esk

shops, a restaurant, a well-being area and toilets. Head through the Yard and turn left towards the corner of the parking area and past the single storey building that once housed the laundry before joining the riverside path into woodland. Pass underneath a treetop rope walking area which is part of a Go Ape facility, before bearing left at the marker and uphill towards a beautiful old oak woodland.

Follow the clear path through this Site of Special Scientific Interest (SSSI) where some of the oak trees are over 900 years old. Kings used to hunt in this forest in days gone by and it still supports a diversity of wildlife. The path ends at the meeting of the River North and River South Esk to form the River Esk. The remains of supports for a footbridge that once crossed the River South Esk it can still be seen.

ESKBANK: WALK 6

Special Oak Trees
Dalkeith Country Park is designed with a mix of grazed forest, arboretum and plantation woodland. The longevity of the Oak Forest has allowed several trees to acquire special status. The Mother Tree provides seedlings that maintain the community of trees within the park, making them healthier and more resistant to climate change. The Michael tree is probably 900 years old and the oldest in the park planted by monks from Melrose in 1150. The Ladies' Seat provided a sheltered spot for ladies from the estate and elsewhere to picnic.

Sites of Special Scientific Interest
Sites of Special Scientific Interest (SSSIs) are areas of land that best represent our natural heritage. They are designated based on unusual collections of plants or animals, rocks or unusual landforms. 12.6% of Scotland's land area consists of SSSIs.

4. Cross the footbridge over the River North Esk and turn right to join the roadway that swings left under a road bridge. Continue ahead on a broad track for a km as it swings right between fields. On meeting a path intersection keep right before descending towards Smeaton Bridge. Continue up the slope into the estate and keep right to join a straight road across the local by-pass back towards Restoration Yard.

Orangery
The Orangery, built in 1832, is a 12-sided conservatory now glassless but still retaining its former grandeur. It was originally used to grow exotic fruits like oranges and figs for the Duke of Buccleuch with the heat provided by boilers that consumed a ton of coal daily.

ESKBANK: WALK 6

5. Pass Go Ape to cross Laundry Bridge, designed by William Adam in 1740. On your left is the Orangery, which once grew oranges and figs. Continue through the courtyard and as you join the entrance road look out for a marker post directing you left onto woodland.

6. Keep on this path to cross the old entrance road to Dalkeith Palace, now a large avenue of grass. Continue on the path to

Smeaton Bridge

the side of St Mary's Episcopal Church, which the suffragettes tried to blow up during their bombing and arson campaign, before heading out the cobbled main entrance of the park. Follow the pavement on the right along the High Street past St Nicholas Buccleuch Parish Church where in 1659 the notorious witchfinder, Reverend Calderwood, became parish minister leading to an increase in those accused of witchcraft with weekly trials held in Dalkeith. Continue through the centre of town, past traffic lights to the pedestrian crossing beside Morrisons supermarket.

7. Cross to the entrance to Kings Park and take the path that runs right before leaving the park through a gap in the wall onto Park Road with its elegant Victorian houses. On reaching the main road turn left and within a few metres cross onto Ancrum Road. Where this ends cross, turn left and continue past Edinburgh College to return to the station.

Oak Trees
An oak tree supports more wildlife ranging from insects, birds, mammals, lichen and fungi than any other native tree and can produce as many as five million acorns over its lifespan. Druids practised rituals in oak groves and kings and Roman emperors wore crowns of oak leaves.

ESKBANK: WALK 7

E7 WATER & BRIDGES

This short stroll takes you along both banks of the beautiful tree-lined waters of the River South Esk and past the impressive Victorian built Newbattle viaduct.

1. Leave the station and head past Edinburgh College and a solar farm to the main road. Turn right and within a few hundred metres cross and enter woodland through the large opening in the wall with a fingerpost to Eskbank. Keep right and drop to the housing estate close to a burn before heading across an area of grassland. With houses on your right continue across the road to the tree line before you.

ESKBANK: *WALK 7*

Newbattle Viaduct
The viaduct remained unused for 43 years after the closure of the Waverley Route and Lady Victoria Colliery. This is the second viaduct to be built here; the original (constructed 1830-32) lay just to the east and some associated

earthworks remain. Costing £22,000, it was wide enough to accommodate two tracks.

2. Head into the woodland and on meeting the metal railing above the River South Esk bear right and follow the broad path through a woodland of oak and yew trees. The lack of ground plants here is due to the density of the yew tree canopy where little grows underneath, only the occasional whitebeam or ash where the sun penetrates. The path turns right up the bank to the side of a field, turn left and continue to the roadside. Opposite is the impressive span of the Newbattle Viaduct which once carried the Waverley Route but now forms part of the Borders Railway to Tweedbank.

3. Keep left past the Sun Inn, an old coaching inn, then take a left turn through the wall opening and bear left to follow the path that runs above the River South Esk. There are significant drops to the river below, so proceed with care. The River South Esk rises on the western slopes of Blackhope Scar in the Moorfoot Hills then flows through Gladhouse and

ESKBANK: **WALK 7**

Coaching Inn
The Sun Inn was on an old coaching route which provided fresh horses for the stagecoaches and refreshments for the driver and passengers. Often noisy places with the clattering of hooves on the cobblestones and the blare of horns announcing the arrival of a coach making sleep difficult.

Roseberry reservoirs before converging with the River North Esk in the grounds of Dalkeith Country Park to form the River Esk. Continue through trees until a set of steps, at the end of a wire fence, that drops left to join the side of Newbattle Road. During autumn an abundance of mushrooms can be found in this woodland.

4. Turn left to recross the River South Esk and beyond the bridge take the first left onto a single-track roadway. Head past housing into the woodland to the riverside and continue until reaching the metal rail encountered earlier. Cross the grass area next to the rear of housing, over the road and into woodland to return up the slope to the road entrance.

5. Cross and turn left and take the first right signposted for Eskbank and follow the track as it swings left over the railway. This is one of 42 new bridges built for the Borders Railway with a further 94 refurbished and brought back into use. Take an immediate right turn onto a grass track that runs above the railway and cross the footbridge to return to the station.

River Esk
The River North Esk has its source in the Pentland Hills near the North Esk reservoir while the River South Esk starts high in the Moorfoot Hills on the side of Blackhope Scar. Both rivers flow towards Dalkeith Country Park where they converge to form the River Esk which flows into the Firth of Forth at Fisherrow.

THE GRAY BROTHER

By Sir Walter Scott
VERSE 11, 12, 16, 17 AND 20

Again unto his native land
His weary course he drew,
To Lothian's fair and fertile strand,
And Pentland's mountains blue.

His unblest feet his native seat,
'Mid Eske's fair woods, regain;
Thro' woods more fair no stream more sweet
Rolls to the eastern main.

From that fair dome, where suit is paid
By blast of bugle free,
To Auchendinny's hazel glade,
And haunted Woodhouselee.

Who knows not Melville's beechy grove,
And Roslin's rocky glen,
Dalkeith, which all the virtues love,
And classic Hawthornden?

It fell upon a summer's eve,
While, on Carnethy's head,
The last faint gleams of the sun's low beams
Had streak'd the grey with red;

NEWTONGRANGE

National Mining Museum

5th Station from Waverley & 4th Station from Tweedbank

Newtongrange (known locally as Nitten) was originally a farm steading before transforming into Scotland's largest mining village in the 1890s, due to its location above the Midlothian Coalfield.

The sinking of the Lady Victoria Colliery, named in honour of the wife of the Marquis of Lothian, marked a significant turning point for the village. It was the deepest mine in Scotland at the time with a shaft sunk to 530m. The colliery closed in 1981 and is now home to the National Mining Museum, one of the best-preserved Victorian Collieries in Europe.

With so many dependent on the employment offered by the mine and the harsh conditions the miners endured, a strong community spirit developed. Their pride is evident from the many memorials throughout the town. Among them, mounted on a pedestal is a statue of a miner. He holds his hard hat in one hand and a shovel in the other, clear symbols of his trade.

The Dean Tavern is one of the few remaining Gothenburg pubs in Scotland. Designed to discourage excessive drinking and to support local causes the tavern was established in 1899 for the local miners and their families. It continues to play an important role in the community.

Welfare Park, as the name suggests, was paid for by the Miners Welfare Fund which was money donated from the miner's wages. It has hosted 'Brass in the Park', and has views of the Pentlands and Arthur's Seat while providing a range of recreational spaces for all.

A striking reminder of the town's history can be seen in the miners' cottages that occupy one side of the High Street. These brick-built houses are laid out on parallel streets named First to Tenth Street. For 40 years, until he died in 1939, the Lady Victoria Colliery manager, Mungo Mackay oversaw the upkeep of the cottages. He carried out regular checks, berating anyone who did not maintain standards!

The disappearance of mining threatened the survival of the town. However, the spirit of those earlier times remains and Newtongrange is still a thriving and prosperous community.

NEWTONGRANGE *WALK 1*

N1 A LIVING PAST

The mysteriously named Povert Road is lined with the oldest form of hedging, Blackthorn, which has been used as a livestock barrier for over 4,500 years. The magnificent 13th century Dalhousie Castle, the oldest inhabited castle in Scotland, has been host to numerous famous guests over the centuries.

1. Take the steps close to the platform to the roadside, turn left, cross the rail bridge then left again and follow the winding footpath as it drops towards a housing estate. Stay right on the footpath under streetlights to the main road through the estate.

2. Keep left and stay on the pavement crossing two road junctions to a bend in the road.

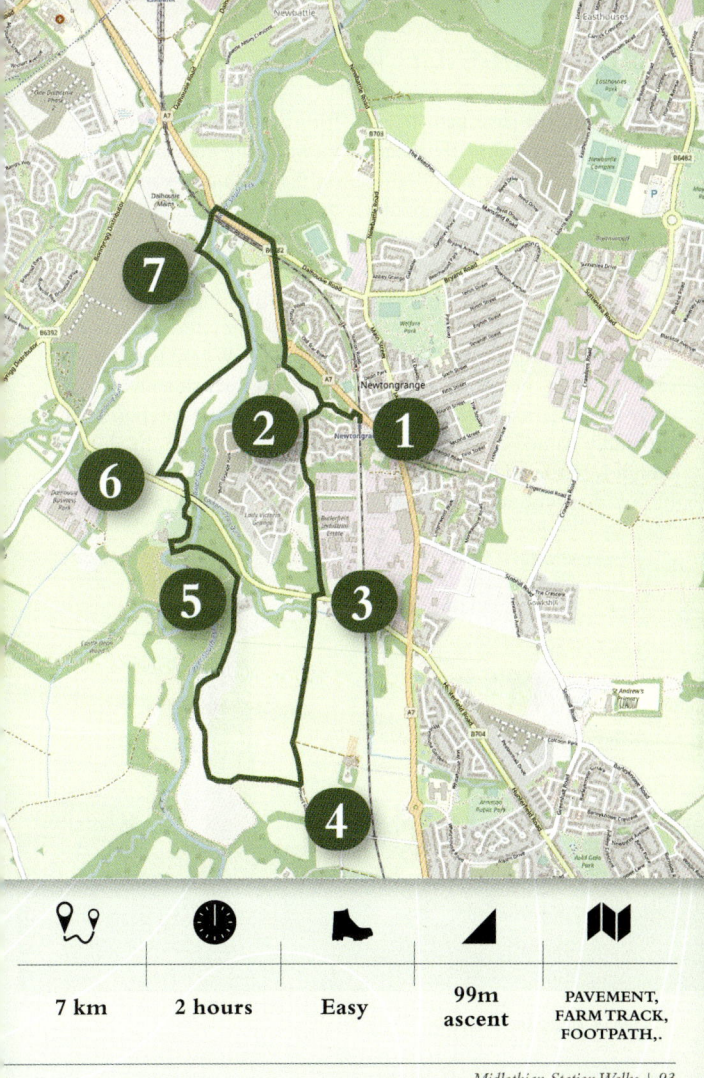

NEWTONGRANGE: *WALK 1*

Turn left on the clear path avoiding the path directly ahead. Beyond a utility box is Butlerfield Industrial Estate, cross the road through the estate and follow the pavement right to the main road, cross and keep right.

3. Beyond Lothian Cat Rescue, turn left onto the path that drops away from the roadside. This is the oddly named Povert Road which is bordered by Blackthorn bushes that produce a purplish fruit called sloes. There are good views to the Pentland Hills and on the skyline to your left the distinctive winding gear of Lady Victoria Colliery.

4. After just under a kilometre look out for a line of trees on your right. Where they join the main track at a metal gate, step around the gatepost, and follow the path up the slope to open ground. The area is abundant in wild roses during the

Victoria Colliery on the skyline

Dalhousie Castle

Dalhousie Castle was built in red sandstone in the 13th century and is sited on a small promontory above the River South Esk. The castle was owned by the Ramsay family for eight centuries before it was sold in 1977 and is now a luxury hotel.

The castle has had numerous important guests over the centuries including Mary, Queen of Scots, Sir Walter Scott and Queen Victoria. Cromwell used it as his headquarters for the invasion of Scotland in 1648.

Several ghosts are said to haunt the castle. The most seen is The Grey Lady who taps on doors and shoulders and hates bagpipe music!

NEWTONGRANGE: **WALK 1**

Archery targets at Dalhousie

summer. Continue ahead before descending right, down banking to an open area, that once served as a car garage. Keep right and stay on this tree covered track as it heads up a slope to an exit gate. Head through and just beyond on your left is a large metal field gate.

5. Enter woodland through the gap next to the gate post and continue across rough ground to join the path that descends under trees to a small bridge. On crossing the bridge, a dramatic view of the magnificent red sandstone building, Dalhousie Castle appears. This is Scotland's oldest inhabited castle. Ascend right, up steps and keep to the tree line and circle the large grass area in front of the castle. Pass a falconry where a variety of birds of prey can be seen, before arriving at the castle road entrance. Cross the entrance road and join the pavement on the left as it winds its way up out of the estate.

6. Just before the public road, turn right onto a single-track road to a disused walled garden containing new houses. Keep left alongside a stone wall and continue on the path that narrows as it edges farmland. The sound of falling water from a large weir on the River South Esk can be heard through the trees before arriving at the road-side next to a cottage.

7. Keep right and join a rough pavement on the opposite side before heading under one of the archways of the magnificently constructed Newbattle Viaduct, built in the 1800's and now carrying the Borders Railway. Cross with great care on this very busy and fast section of road then go right past the Sun Inn, an old coaching inn, and follow the pavement to the traffic lights before crossing right under the viaduct arch. Continue uphill and just before the roundabout cross right and continue to a crossing point beyond the junction. Head over, turn right and within a few metres turn left into parkland. At a path intersection keep left to where the path zigzags up the bank to the main road, turn right and immediately right and down steps to the station.

Blackthorn

Blackthorn is a native species and grows in scrub, copses, and woodland. It has been used for at least 4,500 years as a livestock barrier making it the world's oldest hedging. In March and April, the trees are covered in snow white flowers and later in the year the purplish sloes appear. Sloes can be used to make wine, preserves and of course our favourite winter tipple, sloe gin!

The timber is hard wearing and tough and was traditionally used for making walking sticks. It can also be used as a firewood as it burns slowly with little smoke. It is said that witches' wands and staffs were made from it while witches and heretics were burned on blackthorn pyres.

Midlothian Station Walks | 97

Trees in the grounds of Dalhousie Castle

NEWTONGRANGE *WALK 2*

N2 DISTANT VIEWS

The identity bestowed on this part of Scotland by the industrial age still holds sway as proud reminders of its past are everywhere. A magnificent Victorian viaduct, a statue commemorating an impressive mining past and rows of restored brick-built cottages that did much to improve people's lives.

1. Leave the station up the steps, turn left over the rail bridge and as the pavement ends, cross with care before heading downhill. On passing a roundabout stay on the pavement and continue to traffic lights below the magnificent sandstone Newbattle

NEWTONGRANGE: *WALK 2*

Welfare Park

Welfare Park is a fifteen acre municipal park developed to provide a healthy outdoor environment for the local mining community. It has views of Arthur's Seat and the Pentland Hills and home to a range of recreational and sporting facilities. Lord Chelmsford opened the park in 1926 and it remains an important well used local facility.

Dean Tavern
On the Main Street is the Dean Tavern, established in 1899 and built for the miners and their families who worked in the local collieries. Even now though the mines have gone the Tavern plays an important role in the community. It was based on the Gothenburg principle where drinking is regulated, and the profits re-invested in the local community.

Viaduct. Cross both carriages with care, turn left then after a few metres right through a large wall opening into Lady Lothians Plantation.

2. Keep left on the path that runs above a steep drop and through woodland, covered in wild garlic in spring. As the path swings right alongside a field take the steps down a steep slope to emerge through a gap in the wall to a main road.

3. Turn left before crossing to an

NEWTONGRANGE: *WALK 2*

A winding wheel on Newtongrange's Main Street

old gate entrance, keeping to the right of this, and follow the path up a slope below a high wall. The path swings right before turning left between the wall and a large field. Continue until the wall ends and a metal fence is in front of you then turn right and keep ahead at the rear of housing to the edge of a housing estate.

4. Cross the road, turn left then right into Mansfield Avenue. On meeting Bryan's Avenue keep left onto Bryan's Road and stay right on the pavement to a crossing point to the entrance to the park. Bryans Road was once the site of a short rail branch that served Bryans Pit and continued to a lime works and a quarry beyond.

Continue into Welfare Park, opened in 1926 during the general strike and paid for by the miner's welfare fund. Follow the footpath up the slope and enjoy the views to the Pentland Hills. Cross the park to the gated entrance just beyond the war memorial and onto Main Street. Opposite is the Dean Tavern which was established in 1899 for the miners' and their families.

5. Turn left along Main Street and before the Church, built in 1939 to serve the growing mining community, there is an open space containing a statue on a polished granite pedestal. On top, stands a miner, hard hat in one hand, shovel in the other, a fitting monument to the towns mining heritage.

Past the church are rows of miners' cottages, named First to Tenth Street. Housing was allocated according to rank within the Lady Victoria Colliery. These single storey brick cottages were built following the completion of the colliery in 1896. On meeting the junction with the A7 take the crossing, turn right and head back to the station.

Newbattle Viaduct
This 0.5km long railway viaduct spanning the River South Esk was opened in 1849 by the Edinburgh and Hawick Railway to carry the Waverley Route. It replaced the original viaduct built by the Marquess of Lothian to service his coal pits at Arniston. In 1969 the viaduct was closed to passenger traffic due to the Beeching cuts and to freight traffic in 1972. Only minor repairs were required before being reopened in 2015 for the Borders Railway that now runs between Edinburgh and Tweedbank. It is also known as the Lothianburn, Newtongrange or Dalhousie viaduct.

NEWTONGRANGE *WALK 3*

N3 — UP & UNDER

From above Newtongrange there are spectacular views over the town's distinctive skyline to the Firth of Forth and the Kingdom of Fife beyond. The bings that once scarred this landscape have taken on a new life having been transformed into green spaces and woodland where nature now thrives.

1. Leave the station along the entrance road and keep right to the traffic lights. Cross and turn right into Main Street before immediately crossing to the pavement behind the colliery wheel. These were used in mines to deliver men and equipment to the coal seams deep underground. Keep right and take the second

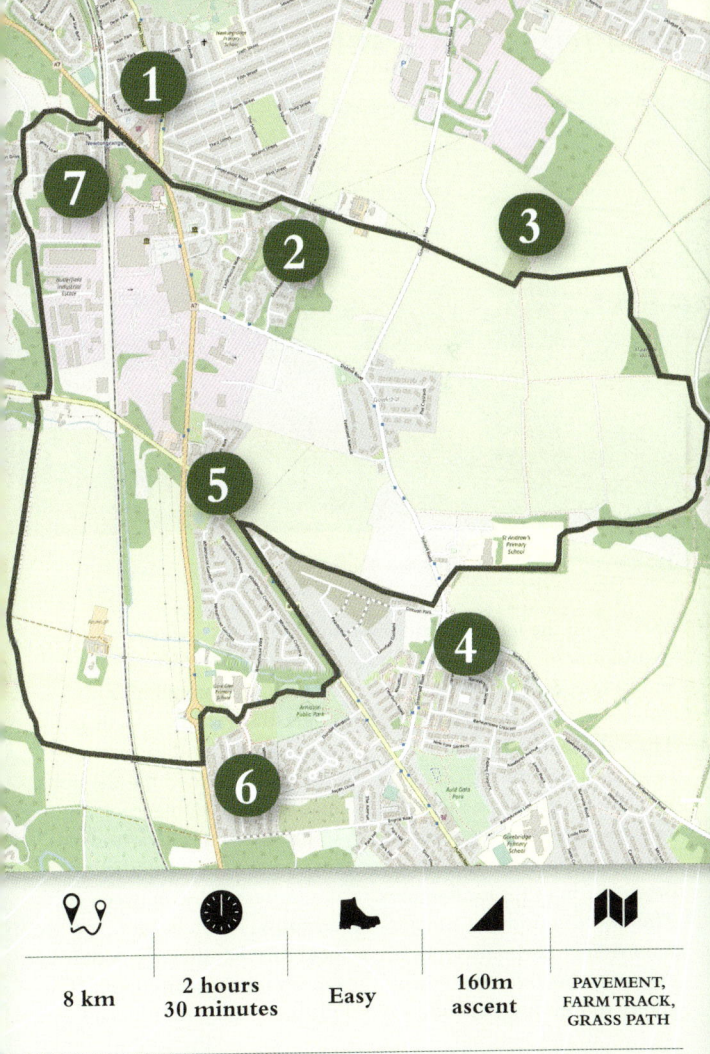

NEWTONGRANGE: *WALK 3*

Looking over to the Pentland Hills from Masterton Wood

opening on the left and head up steps signposted for Camp Wood and Bryans Wood.

The steps swing right onto banking with housing on either side. On reaching the footpath, keep left to exit onto a road lined with single storey brick cottages originally built for local miners. They were considered a major improvement from previous dwellings, however, the miners' ability to care for them was questioned by many!

2. Turn right uphill on a single-track road, through a metal barrier, and past farm steadings. On reaching the public road follow the fingerpost for Camp Wood to join a roadway that narrows to a path before continuing uphill between tall enclosing beech hedges. At a large field turn left then right, onto the farm track that runs uphill. Where a large hedge joins the track from

Firth of Forth Tunnel
Miners once dug a tunnel under the Firth of Forth to link Kinneil Colliery at Bo'ness with Valleyfield in Fife. At five kilometres long, the tunnel operated between 1962 and 1982 before the shafts were capped with concrete. The tunnel is believed to have collapsed or filled with water. Strange to think that not long-ago people could walk from the Lothians to Fife under the dark waters of the Forth!

the right, take the path on the left of it towards Masterton Wood.

Head directly through the trees before emerging to join a path that you follow uphill. It swings right but remains a few metres from the field boundary. Fine views of the Firth of Forth appear and beyond, on a clear day, the Ochil Hills! On arriving onto a raised piece of ground, turn left into an old slag heap strewn with debris. Slag heaps, or bings, are often colonised by the short-lived pioneer species, such as silver birch that can live in mineral-poor soils.

3. Turn right and take the first exit from this rough ground into trees and follow the path downhill. On leaving the tree cover, the path drops next to a large field and on meeting a fence line follow the path left. Continue ahead to a fingerpost for Greenhall which takes you along tree lined track to a fence that borders St Andrew's Primary School.

4. On arriving at the main road, keep left on the pavement for about 100m. Look out for a path on the opposite side that runs between hedging and newly built houses before crossing with care to join it. Continue to the end of the housing estate to a fenced area containing a Sustainable Drainage System, used to manage stormwater from the estate. Take the path in the lower corner beside a wall and continue downhill to the main road.

NEWTONGRANGE: *WALK 3*

The track down towards St Andrews Primary School

5. Turn left uphill to where the tree line opposite ends and a row of houses begins. Cross the road with care and head into Arniston Park. Great views of the Pentland Hills are to be had from here. Take the footpath downhill past football courts before negotiating the crossing to the side of Gore Glen Primary School. Turn left and at the junction cross to the other side before turning right to the roundabout.

6. Keep left on the pavement and take the first turning on the right onto a single-track road to head over a rail bridge and on through a metal gate signposted for Butlerfield Industrial Estate. This is the oddly named Povert Road whose name probably dates back to the 17th century and derives from the nearby Butlerfield which at one time was called Polvart Maynes meaning 'the steading on the stream'. Continue along this track between fields that narrows to a path ending at the roadside. Cross with care into Butlerfield Industrial Estate and follow the pavement past a barrier into a housing estate.

7. Keep right and after crossing two road entrances and when the housing ends, turn right down the slope and follow the footpath under lampposts to the far corner of this area of grassland. Head up to the roadside on a winding footpath, turn right and return down the steps to the station.

Coal
Coal has been mined in and around Newtongrange for generations. The founding of the Lothian Coal company towards the end of the 19th century allowed these deposits to be exploited using modern methods. The colliery site was chosen because of easy access to the Edinburgh – Carlisle railway and proximity to the Lingerwood Colliery where an underground connection could be made between both mines, a legal requirement at the time.

GOREBRIDGE

Borthwick Church

6th Station from Waverley & 3rd Station from Tweedbank

Gorebridge was founded by the Dewar family who lived at Vogrie House. It got its name from the bridge across the Gore Water, a tributary of the River South Esk. With a population of approximately 8,000, it has a commanding view across the valley to the Pentland Hills and was a popular holiday destination in the 19th century.

Stobsmill was Scotland's first gunpowder works and began operations on the banks of the Gore Water in 1794 where four dams and ten waterwheels powered the machinery. The Napoleonic Wars produced an increase in production as Britain needed as much gunpowder as it could get.

The town grew servicing the surrounding farms and the gunpowder works and greatly increased in size following the opening of the railway in 1847. It developed further with the opening of Emily and Gore pits in 1874, which were later renamed the Arniston Colliery before closing in 1962.

Main Street has undergone a lot of changes over the years but has retained the typical character of a Victorian village. It is a designated Conservation Area to preserve its historic and architectural past.

There was a corn mill at Catcune which was established in 1620 and grew into a substantial operation by the mid-19th century with a large stone-built granary next to the railway. The mill closed in 1979 with the older mill buildings and granary converted to domestic use.

Annie Shepherd Swan, a writer of romantic fiction, suffragette and founder member of the Scottish National Party had a home in Gorebridge. The long-suffering wife of Victor Meldrew in the BBC comedy series "One Foot in the Grave", Annette Crosbie, is a former resident of the town.

GOREBRIDGE *WALK 1*

G1 MOVING THROUGH TIME

The area's long history is everywhere to be seen. With a medieval castle and church and close by a standing stone linked to close encounters with aliens and strange nocturnal occurrences!

1. Leave the station and head downhill to the road junction, cross to the opening directly in front of you and follow the track along Robertson Bank. On meeting Scally's Motor Spares yard keep to the path that runs alongside it. At a narrow bridge keep left and follow the track as it swings right past some houses, one of which belonged to the writer of romantic fiction, Annie Shepherd Swan.

| 7.5 km | 2 hours | Moderate | 141m ascent | PAVEMENT, WOODLAND PATH, ROAD, FOOTPATH |

Midlothian Station Walks | 117

GOREBRIDGE: *WALK 1*

2. Past the houses enter woodland and follow the way marker right into a field through a kissing gate. Head left along the field and on passing a weir head up the bank and through another kissing gate to the next field. Continue down the slope past a large depression in the landscape, where the 14th century Catcune Castle once stood. Leave the field in the lower corner through a gate passing close to the water's edge and through another field to the road. Over the bridge, a corn mill was established in 1620 which grew into a substantial operation by the mid-19th century. It closed in 1979 with the older mill buildings and granary converted into domestic properties.

3. Cross the road and over the stile with a signpost for Gore Way and Borthwick. Continue alongside the water to two bridge supports that once carried a railway transporting lime from the nearby Esperton Lime Quarry to the Waverley Route. Head up the banking, turn left and follow the curve of the old railway towards a brick building and the gate beyond. Pass through then turn left next to a fence and continue to the field gate in the far corner with Borthwick Castle and Church appearing in the distance.

4. Turn right alongside the fence to a small gate, enter and turn left before the path starts to climb along banking to woodland. Take two stepping boards onto the track running between the deer fence and trees. As this short section ends take the stile into the next field. Keep right and within 100m take a stepping board into a strip of woodland that runs alongside the river and continue left to a further stile to the roadside.

5. Turn right and follow the road as it gradually swings uphill before taking a sharp left to Borthwick Castle, sitting on a small hill with steep drops on three sides. Unusually, it retains many of the narrow windows from when it was built in 1439. Directly in front sits Borthwick

Borthwick Church

Borthwick Parish Church has been here since the 12th century (medieval times) with the addition of the Arniston Isle in the 15th and a Gothic Revival spire in the 19th century. The first church was very simple, built sometime before 1153, known then as "Lochfeureur" and dedicated to St. Kentigern (also known as St. Mungo).

GOREBRIDGE: **WALK 1**

Annie Shepherd Swan
Annie Shepherd Swan was a journalist and writer of romantic fiction publishing over 200 novels, stories, serials, and other fiction. 'Aldersyde' was her first successful novel in 1883 which was also the name of her Gorebridge home. She was a suffragette, liberal activist and founding member and vice president of the SNP.

Church, a site of Christian worship since the 9th century.

After visiting the church grounds (not possible for the castle), retrace your steps back to the last field or take the concrete steps next to the castle entrance and head down the field to the roadside and turn right.

6. Stay on the winding road for 2km crossing the railway and head uphill to the crossroads. A small standing stone, which can be easily missed, sits in the hawthorn hedge on the right-hand side of the road before the crossroads. Its original use is a mystery, but it may have been a boundary marker or

Catcune Mill

A gargoyle on Borthwick Church

have some connection with the ancient track which is now the present-day road. According to local news reports the stone has seen several odd events such as close encounters with aliens and strange nocturnal lights[1]

Continue ahead past Wrights House Farm on the top of Gallows Hill where great views open over this rich arable land towards the Moorfoot and Pentland Hills before the road begins to descend.

7. Look out for a fingerpost on your left that directs you onto Gorebridge Circular Path. Take the steps into a section of rough grassland and continue downhill between fields to a small gate below which lies a single-track road. Turn right and on reaching the main road, cross to a footpath beyond a hedge and follow it downhill to a metal barrier.

Head downhill and where the pavement ends cross to the other side. Continue to just beyond the rail bridge before crossing the road with care to the entrance of St Margaret's Catholic Church and take the steps down to the station.

GOREBRIDGE *WALK 2*

G2 AN EXPLOSIVE PAST

Immerse yourself in the area's explosive past and navigate Scotland's first gunpowder mill located in Gore Glen. Powered by the waters of the mighty Gore it supplied Britain's forces during the Napoleonic Wars.

1. Leave the station and head downhill to the road junction before crossing right to the opposite pavement then left over the bridge and on arriving at a bus stop turn right onto the narrow path. At the path junction signposted, Gorebridge Circular Walk, turn right into a housing estate. Continue past a fingerpost into John Bernard Way and join the path that runs between

GOREBRIDGE: *WALK 2*

Stobmills Gunpowder Factory
Scotland's first gunpowder mill began operations on the banks of the Gore Water in 1794 and with the Napoleonic Wars there was enormous demand for gunpowder. The expanding coal industry and quarries were also large consumers of gunpowder. Four dams on the Gore Water drove ten waterwheels to operate the machinery. Different departments within the mills were separated by mounds of earth and trees to minimise any destruction in the event of an explosion.

houses to the parking area next to the sports field.

2. To the left of the Arniston Rangers YFC Pavilion, next to the fence, a fingerpost directs you across the playing fields to a stone wall. Where the wall ends enter a field, turn right and follow the edge of the field to woodland. Take the steps down the bank past the derelict remains of Stobmills, Scotland's first gunpowder mill, embedded into the hillside. Turn left alongside Gore Water under a covering of trees before the path narrows as it enters scrubland to arrive at the main road.

3. Turn right over the bridge past the memorial, built with stones from the original 1797 bridge and decorative iron finials from

Stone bridge over the Gore Water

GOREBRIDGE: *WALK 2*

The path from Gore Glen

its predecessor. As Shanks Bridge ends take an immediate right over the crash barrier into woodland at the fingerpost for Gorebridge Circular Walk.

4. At the top of the steps descend to Gore Water with Shanks Bridge appearing above you through the trees. Continue under the bridge, keeping left at the only junction, before dropping to the side of Gore Water. On passing a pond, almost permanently covered in green algae, continue through open woodland above the river to an old stone bridge.

5. Cross and within 20m turn left up the bank and follow the path through this airy woodland with a mixture of conifer and broadleaf trees. Broadleaf trees, like ash, oak, sycamore and beech are native to the UK, while most conifers are non-native except for yew, juniper and Scots pine. At the side of the field, bear left before crossing between deer fences and continuing left to the wide track next to a storage area. Head downhill past the old entrance to Arniston House with an ornate metal gate and lodges on either side. Lodges were added to country mansions in the eighteenth and nineteenth centuries, mostly designed to deter intruders. Continue to the main road and cross with care to re-join the path used earlier and retrace your steps back to the station.

Graffiti on the Shanks Bridge

Shanks Bridge
Two previous bridges spanning the Gore Water stood here on this site, built respectively in 1802 and 1901. The latter was an iron and stone structure taking the A7 trunk road over the Gore Water and was demolished 1977/78. A memorial was built using stone from the original 1797 bridge which contained a plaque, now missing, that depicted the history of the early bridges.

GOREBRIDGE *WALK 3*

G3 BRIDGES & RIVERS

Discover the beautiful and diverse woodland that lines the banks of two rivers while passing a reminder of recent industrial strife and the lair of a former cattle thief! Walk through the grounds of a Medieval hunting park with connections to royalty and the foremost Scottish architect of the 18th century.

1. Leave the station and head downhill to the road junction. Cross right to the pavement opposite before turning left over the road bridge and at the bus stop turn right again onto the narrow path. At the intersection signposted for Gorebridge

GORBRIDGE: *WALK 3*

Choosing Stobmills Site
Safety considerations dictated both the location and layout of the Stobmills gunpowder works. The site was isolated and secluded and the steep elongated valley allowed the 30 or so buildings to be spread across a wide area. The Gore Water supplied the power that manufacturing required and proximity to Leith docks and the Waverley Route meant that raw materials such as saltpetre and sulphur could be easily imported. While the mills closed in 1861, some ruins still remain in woodland by Gore Water.

Circular Walk turn right into a housing estate. Continue past a fingerpost into John Bernard Way to join the path running between houses that leads to the parking area next to a sports field.

2. To the left of the Arniston Rangers YFC Pavilion, next to the fence, a fingerpost directs you across the playing fields to a stone wall. Where the wall ends at a fingerpost enter the field and turn right to the woodland below. Take the steps down the banking and past the remains of Stobmills, Scotland's first gunpowder mill, embedded into the hillside. Turn left alongside Gore Water and continue along the path to the main road.

Turn right, cross Shanks Bridge and on reaching the other side step over the crash barrier and follow signs for Gorebridge Circular Walk. At steps set into the bank, follow these to the side of Gore Water and under the road bridge and on through woodland. The graffiti-covered legs of the bridge are either an eye sore or a delight! Keep left at a small junction and continue to where the path swings right past a small pond with the river below.

3. At an old stone bridge, close to the confluence of Gore Water and the River South Esk, cross and follow the path that runs next to the River South Esk as it meanders through this scenic glen. The large weir and associated buildings were built to provide hydroelectric power to the Arniston Estate during the miners' strike in 1983. While

Arniston House
The Arniston Estate is over 6,000 acres and was a royal hunting park during the Middle Ages. It was also owned by the Knights Templar who gave the nearby village of Temple its name. The estate was bought by the Dundas family in 1571 who have been in residence for over 450 years. The Dundas's have played a role in Scottish affairs for centuries, many of whom were judges and politicians. The current Arniston House was designed and built by the Scottish architect William Adams and is open for guided tours from May to September.

GOREBRIDGE: *WALK 3*

Kings Cave

Gorebridge was plunged into darkness the lights of Arniston House stayed on.

After just under a km, past the large field guarded by deer fencing, there is a prominent rocky sandstone outcrop, containing an opening called Kings Cave. According to legend, it was used as a hiding place by a cattle thief, and not as some believe, named after Robert the Bruce!

Cross the stone bridge, bear right, and follow the winding path up the bank with farmland appearing on your right and the Pentland Hills on the horizon.

Continue ahead for some distance passing under a stand of mature beech trees until the path drops to the River South Esk.

Keep right, staying close to the river, towards a stone bridge, cross and continue over the open field to a route marker with a large conifer opposite, then left up the steep bank to the grounds of Arniston House. The path is blocked by tree trunks that require a short scramble along the bank to pass.

4. At the top head through an open storage area and then left through trees and past Arniston House. The Royal Coat of Arms of Scotland appears above the main doorway of the house and may have come from Parliament House in Edinburgh after renovations in the 1800s.

Just beyond the house, turn left onto the farm track and continue for just over a km. After crossing the second of two small bridges pass through a farm gate and take an immediate right to enter a field with a farmhouse ahead of you.

5. Before the exit gate from the field turn left onto the farm track that crosses the field. This is Arniston Mains Farm which has a dairy herd, and the fields need to be avoided when the cows are being taken for milking. The land had been depleted by industrial use as it was once an open cast mine, before undergoing a system of renewal that led to a healthier and more productive soil that now produces high-quality meat and dairy.

Continue across two more fields to Harvieston Mains House and follow the track to the main road before crossing with care. Turn right and where a line of trees begins take the gap in the wall towards the side of the football field. Cross directly to the Pavilion or take the path around the side of the field if a game is in progress. Head through the housing estate and retrace your route back to the station.

GOREBRIDGE *WALK 4*

G4 TOWN OF THE WARRIORS

Walk in the footsteps of the Knights Templar whose stronghold in Scotland for many centuries was Temple Church. Imagine these 'warriors' travelling through this ancient landscape with its dramatic gorges and fast-flowing rivers.

1. Head along the platform and take the steps to the road above before crossing with care to join the wide track opposite above the railway. At the footbridge head downhill through woodland then left over a stile and into the field.

2. Take the path that runs alongside the fence next to the Gore Water and at a weir head up a short steep bank to an exit

GOREBRIDGE: *WALK 4*

gate into the next field. Catcune Castle, built in the 14th century as a fortified residence once stood here, a depression in the land shows its original site. Continue to the corner and navigate the path above the water's edge before crossing the next field to join a minor road.

3. Turn right past Catcune Mill, where the old sandstone mill stones can still be seen, and after approximately 500m arrive at the side of the main road. Turn left on the pavement and after passing a layby two large field gates appear on the other side of the road. Cross with care, head through the gates to join the

Catcune Mill

A corn mill was established here in 1620 and grew into a substantial operation by the mid 19th century with a large stone-built granary next to the railway. The mill closed in 1979 with the older mill buildings and granary were converted to domestic use. Waterpower was the dominant power source for mills until steam provided a viable alternative. Windmills pre-dated watermills with the earliest Scottish mill in Largo, Fife, in the mid-15th century.

field track and continue until it begins to disappear, then follow the fence line to the corner of the field.

4. Take the clear crossing point over the fence and up the embankment to join the wide track called the Carlisle Approach Track. Continue as it swings right before joining the road through a large gate with the entrance to Arniston House and its tree-lined road opposite. Turn left on the narrow, and in parts uneven, pavement until the junction opposite a smaller gated entrance to Arniston House.

Cross with care and continue left on the narrow pavement to the road junction. From here the road begins to rise towards Temple Village, take care on this short section as there is no pavement. At the bend head downhill to find a gap in the wall with a fingerpost indicating Gore Glen. Just below this point, a short detour will take you to Temple Old Kirk which is well worth a visit.

5. Drop to the edge of the River South Esk and stay on the path, under the 1930s reinforced concrete Braidwood Bridge, to an area dominated by large beech trees. Bear right to cross an old stone bridge then left into the grounds of Arniston House to an impressive stand of Redwood trees before the path drops down a bank to a large field.

Continue ahead to cross a stone bridge into the next field, keeping right on the path as it runs close to the river. On entering woodland, through cut tree trunks, turn left up banking and through an area of large beech trees. The path runs close to farmland with impressive views of the Pentland Hills to your left before dropping to flatter ground and then on to cross the River South Esk. Stay ahead next to the river as it cuts its way back and forth through the glen.

6. Cross the bridge above the confluence of the Gore Water and the River South Esk keeping

GOREBRIDGE: *WALK 4*

Temple Church
Temple Church dates back to the 12th century. Formerly called Balantrodoch, meaning the 'town of the warriors' in Scottish Gaelic and was the principal seat of the Knights Templar in Scotland. There are many interesting headstones in the churchyard including a memorial to John Craig who died in 1742 and is carved in his best clothing alongside his two children.

right past a marker on the track that runs above the Gore Water, this is Gore Glen Woodland Park. Continue along the wide track for a km before it swings right to pass a small pond before bearing left under Shanks Bridge. Take the steps up the steep bank and continue to the footbridge over the railway.

7. Turn right on the other side to join the footpath and where this ends follow the path ahead before it swings right through scrubland to a gate leading to a housing estate. Stay ahead before turning right to leave the estate on the footpath that passes close to what little remains of the 16th century Newbyres Castle. Continue past Newbyres Nursery to the main road, turn right and cross to the opposite pavement before continuing downhill to the station.

Braidwood Bridge
Braidwood Bridge was built in the 1930s from reinforced concrete and spans high over the River South Esk. The bridge has incorporated the parapets of the earlier bridge built in 1811 which it replaced.

GOREBRIDGE *WALK 5*

G5 — CIRCLE OF PITCHES

Football fields and a recreational area have arisen in this man-made amphitheatre from the site of the old Arniston Colliery. The remains of an even older structure conjure up images of more ancient times but even then, coal was king!

1. Leave the station and head uphill along the Main Street with its traditional Victorian sandstone buildings, dating from the late 19th century, stepping up the street. The town has 29 listed buildings including Gorebridge Station. On arriving in Hunters Square turn left past Newbyres Nursery, which is housed in an impressively renovated old church, and walk past the car

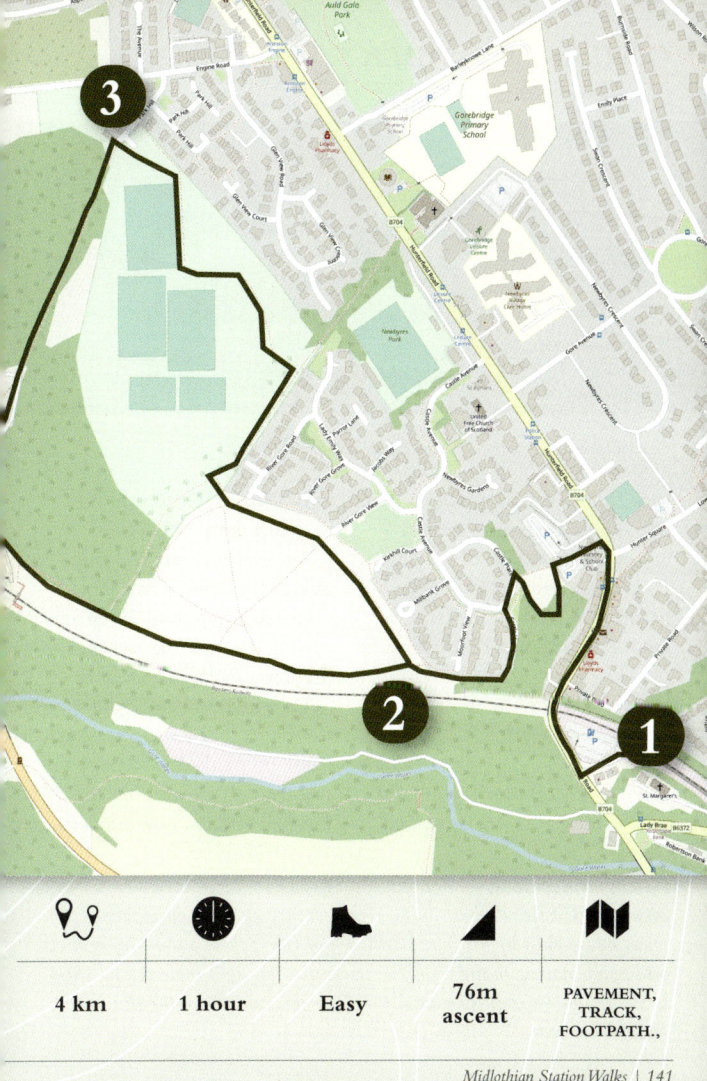

GOREBRIDGE: **WALK 5**

Gorebridge Parish Church from the football fields

park to join the footpath on your left. There is an information board giving details of Newbyres Castle, the remains of which sit before you. Follow the path that circles the site to a housing estate, turn left to join the roadway then left again down the slope to the wooden barrier.

2. Pass through the barrier and follow the path over scrubland until it turns left to join the footpath next to fencing. Continue to where the path swings right and pass a large house to a junction. Keep ahead, passing through the barrier to the side of a large area of football fields which was once the site of the Emily and Gore pits which made up Arniston Colliery. The slag heap that overlooks the football pitches, now tree covered,

Newbyres Castle
Newbyres Castle was built in the 16th century and was an L shaped tower house built by Michael Borthwick of Glengelt to oversee his coal mining operations in the area. The tower was largely demolished in 1963 by Midlothian Council because it was unsafe and little of the structure remains today.

is a reminder of what once took place here.

3. Continue past metal shipping containers to pick up the footpath on your right that runs alongside the rear of housing. Follow this as it winds its way around the park to a tree lined track, close to houses. Keep right and as the houses end drop left into scrub land.

Follow the edge of this area back to the wooden barrier you used earlier. Keep ahead before turning right as the road enters the estate proper, staying on the wide footpath with the remains of Newbyres Castle on your right. Continue past Newbyres Nursery, turn right into Main Street and downhill to the station.

Arniston Colliery
Arniston Colliery was composed of two older pits, the Emily and the Gore. The 293m timber lined shaft was said to be the deepest in Scotland at the time, and at one point the site had its own power station. To help improve conditions for the men who worked there, in 1936 a remarkable system of circular pithead baths was completed at the cost of £12,000.

Looking over from Gorebridge towards the Pentland Hills

GOREBRIDGE *WALK 6*

G6 A WITCHES TALE

An eccentric lady, Margaret Hawthorn *(Meg)*, legendary for her skill with animals lived in Camp Wood which was occupied in Roman times and used as a lookout point during the Napoleonic Wars. It was also a stopping point for cattle drovers and a site for bell pits which were used at one point to extract coal.

1. Leave the station car park and head uphill along the Victorian Main Street of Gorebridge to Hunters Square. Newbyres Nursery is on your left, housed in an old church. Built in 1858 as a Free Church, it became the village hall in 1882 and then, after alterations, a Masonic Lodge in the 1970's.

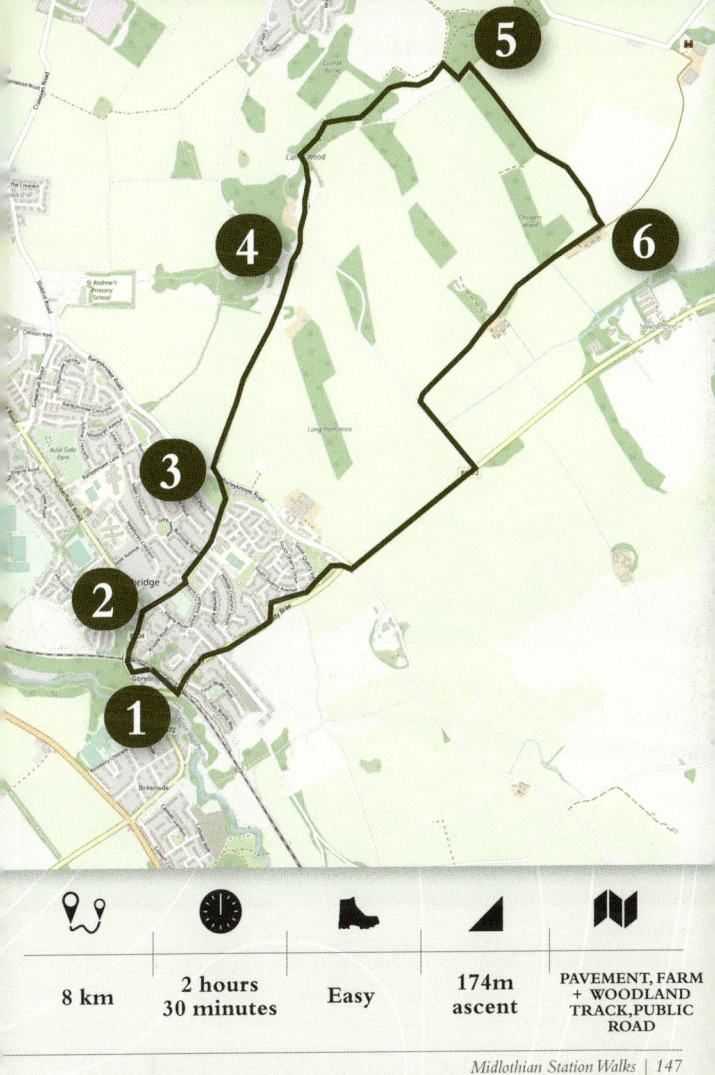

Midlothian Station Walks | 147

GOREBRIDGE: *WALK 6*

Pentland Hills
The Pentland Hills are around 30km (20 miles) in length, and they run southwest from Edinburgh. The highest peak is Scald Law at 579m (1900 feet) which is composed of volcanic rock from about 410 million years ago.

2. Take the road opposite and continue up Hunter Square to the junction with Bonnybank Court. In front is an area of grass with a clear path taking you to Hillside Crescent North. Cross the road and almost immediately, turn right uphill on Bonnybank Road past Stobhill Primary School. On meeting a bend in the road take the path directly ahead into trees and continue uphill. As the path bears left a large communication tower appears opposite on your right and marks the point where a narrow path leads out to the road.

3. Cross the road, turn left then immediately right, through a gate onto a wide track that runs uphill through a field next to a narrow strip of trees. Continue to the brow of the hill where panoramic views take in the Pentland Hills, Moorfoot Hills, Firth of Forth and the ancient volcano that is Arthur's Seat, said to be one of the possible locations for Camelot. These fields were once the site of Blinkbonny Mine which was an opencast coal mine, part of the Midlothian Coalfield stretching towards the Pentlands. It shut in the 1990's and the land restored to farming. Leave the last field to the track that runs between the animal enclosures of Camp Wood Farm.

4. Head through the farm entrance and continue on the road before bearing left alongside more animal enclosures containing geese, goats, donkeys, and Highland cattle. Where the parking area ends, take the gate into woodland, and follow the track with fences on either side through trees. On leaving this area turn right up the slope before heading left towards woodland.

5. Leave the field over the stile and join the path right as indicated by the fingerpost that edges Camp Wood. The wood was once home to Margaret Hawthorn, otherwise known as Camp Meg, a fugitive from Galloway, who allegedly shot her neighbour dead. It was also the site of an ancient hill fort, a

GOREBRIDGE: *WALK 6*

stopping point for cattle drovers and the site of primitive 'bell' pits. Continue around the trees to join the path that drops downhill alongside a fence. In the distance is Berwick Law, a volcanic plug and Traprain Law, a whaleback lump of volcanic rock, reminders of our turbulent geological history.

6. On meeting the fingerpost (Moss Cott ¾ mile) go right past the sawmill, old farm buildings and Blinkbonny Farm, a Category C listed building built in 1839. At the road, turn left and within a few hundred metres you arrive at the B3272. Turn right onto the pavement to the road junction then right past some

Camp Meg
Meg set up home in an abandoned cottage in Camp Wood, a lookout point during the Napoleonic Wars. She dressed like a man and rode a white horse called 'Screwball' and had a reputation for caring for sick animals, her help often sought by local farmers. Meg told stories of confronting the Devil and because of these tales became known as a witch called Camp Meg. During a winter storm in 1827 she died, and her body was found on her doorstep covered in snow.

cottages and quickly left. Almost immediately leave the roadside onto the path that heads towards housing before turning downhill to where the path re-joins the road. Keep right on the pavement and where it ends cross to the other side before continuing downhill. On crossing the rail-bridge, head over the road to the entrance of St Margaret's Catholic Church and take the steps to the station.

A Boer goat grazing at Camp Wood Farm

Open Cast Mining
Open cast mining is where the top few metres of soil were removed so that the coal beneath the surface can be extracted. Increasing costs and environmental concerns have led to the disappearance of open cast mining in Scotland. The last open cast mine closed in Ayrshire in 2020.

GOREBRIDGE *WALK 7*

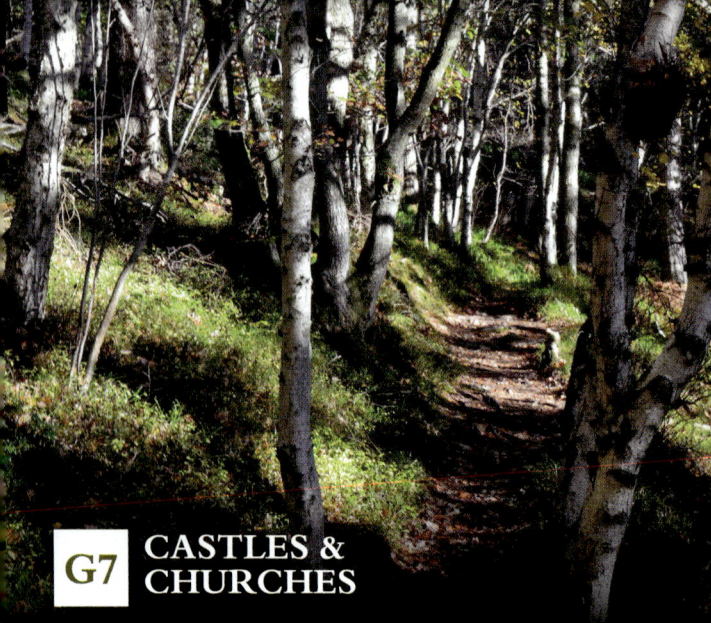

G7 CASTLES & CHURCHES

This walk will test your fitness while firing your imagination with its high vistas, beguiling valleys and industrial relics. Castles and churches occupy prominent positions in the landscape and still show the damage inflicted by war centuries ago.

1. Leave the station and head downhill to the road junction, then cross to the opening opposite and follow the track along Robertson Bank. On meeting Scally's Motor Spares yard keep to the path that runs alongside it. At a narrow bridge, keep left and follow the track as it swings right past some houses,

GOREBRIDGE: *WALK 7*

one of which belonged to the writer of romantic fiction, Annie Shepherd Swan.

2. Enter the woodland and follow the way marker right into the field through the kissing gate. Head left along the field and on passing a weir, head up the banking and through another kissing gate into the next field. Continue down the slope past a large depression in the landscape, where the 14th century Catcune Castle once stood. Leave the field in the lower corner through a gate and pass close to the water's edge to exit the next field onto the road. At the other side of the bridge, a corn mill was established in 1620 and grew into a substantial operation by the mid-19th century. It closed in 1979 with the older mill buildings and granary converted into domestic properties.

3. Cross the road and over the stile signposted for Gore Way and Borthwick. Continue along the side of the water to two bridge supports that once carried the railway transporting lime from the nearby Esperton Lime Quarry to the Waverley Route. Head up the banking, turn left and follow the curve of the old railway embankment towards a brick building and the gate beyond. Pass through this gate then turn left alongside a fence and continue to the field gate in the far corner where Borthwick Castle and Church appear in the distance.

4. Head through and then turn right alongside the fence to a small gate, go through and turn left before the path starts to climb up banking to woodland. Take two stepping boards onto the track which runs between a deer fence and trees. At the end of this section take the stile into the next field and after less than 100m take a stepping board on the right into a strip of woodland that runs alongside the water to another stile to the side of the road.

5. Turn right and follow the road as it swings uphill before taking

Borthwick Castle

Borthwick Castle is one of the largest and best-preserved Scottish medieval fortifications, built in 1430. Mary, Queen of Scots visited the castle twice and was besieged there in 1567 but managed to escape, disguised as a page. During the Civil War in 1650, Cromwell attacked the castle which surrendered after only a few cannon shots. The damage they caused is still visible today. The castle is now an exclusive-use venue.

GOREBRIDGE: *WALK 7*

Crichton Castle
Crichton Castle was built in the late 14th century as a home for the Crichton noble family. It was constructed from sandstone which was quarried locally and sits on a terrace high above the Tyne Water. Mary, Queen of Scots stayed at the castle for 2 years after her marriage to her half cousin Henry Stuart, Lord Darnley, in 1565. Francis Stewart who was inspired by Italian architecture added a diamond-faceted façade to the internal wall overlooking the courtyard which can still be seen today. Francis also had the stable complex built next to the castle which is now home to roosting bats.

a sharp left towards Borthwick Castle and Church. At the entrance to Borthwick Castle turn right past the church and as the short roadway ends head through the gate. Follow the path downhill, cross the footbridge and head out to the roadside. Continue downhill and cross Currie Bridge, taking the path right next to the bridge with a fingerpost indicating Crichton Castle.

6. Continue alongside the burn and through two wooden gates to begin a climb up banking into woodland. At the top a fingerpost directs you left for Crichton Castle. Follow the path uphill for a few metres before entering the field on your left over a stepping board. Almost immediately views of the castle and the Pentland Hills appear in the distance.

Keep right up the bank to high ground and continue before descending through a field and over a stile and a bridge across the railway into birch trees, an area known as Birky Side. This was once a quarry and gravel pit used by the nearby St Margaret's shed as a dumping ground for ash from the steam locomotives. The land has now been returned to nature but there is still evidence of railway debris lying about.

On leaving the trees the path descends through bracken alongside a fence to rough grassland below. Continue towards the infant Tyne Water, which rises in the Moorfoot Hills, and alongside it before crossing a small wooden bridge. Alder trees line the banks here and were used to make charcoal for gunpowder at the nearby Stobmills Gunpowder Mill in Gorebridge.

Keep left and follow the path as it starts to rise towards the castle. You will emerge close to a ruined stable block, which is often mistaken for a chapel. Crichton Castle was built in the late 14th century, is now a ruin and lies beyond. Follow the path past the stable block and the castle

Crichton Castle

GORE BRIDGE: *WALK 7*

Scarlet Elf Cup
Scarlet Elf Cup, also known as moss cup or fairies' bath is a stunning if uncommon fungi. It can be seen from early winter to early spring on decaying branches of Elm, Hazel, or Willow. It pokes through the moss and leaf litter on the woodland floor where it adds a welcome splash of colour. According to folklore wood elves are said to drink morning dew from the cups.

downhill to the parking area. At the time of writing both these structures are fenced off as they are unsafe.

Ahead is Crichton Collegiate Church which was founded in 1449 and built by the Crichton family who paid priests to pray for their family's salvation. On some of the outer walls, the impact marks caused by Cromwell's troops firing their muskets at the church in 1650 can be seen.

7. Head into the parking area and look out for a short section of steps on your left that takes you back towards the castle. As the path ends a fingerpost directs you down the slope and back along a line of impressive beech trees and down steps to a single-track road. Head uphill where you will see the remains of a lime kiln on your right. The abundance of coal in the local area made the production of lime economically possible. The limestone was heated in the kilns by burning coal to produce lime which was then used in buildings and as a fertiliser. Just beyond, take the farm track on your left where brightly coloured Scarlet Elf Cups can sometimes be seen poking through the leaf litter.

Continue on this track to where a sign for Vogrie House appears attached to a tree on your left. Head down a set of steps to the waterside. Cross the wooden bridge over the Tyne Water and turn right alongside the stream until you meet a bridge with Vogrie House signposted to your left. Head across duckboards and up the bank into the grounds of Vogrie House and past the tearoom towards the pond opposite. The baronial mansion was built for the Dewar family in 1875 and is now owned by Midlothian Council. Pass the pond on the left and continue to where a fingerpost directs you through the car park towards the estate exit. Just before another fingerpost directs you left for Newlandrig.

Follow this path into woodland, parallel to the main road, crossing a minor road before continuing to another road with a house opposite. Turn right to the main road, cross with care and turn left on the pavement to the fingerpost next to a house that directs you to Camp Wood.

8. Follow this path on a slow gradual ascent through woodland and alongside fields to Camp Wood, then left through the gate onto the path that circles the woodland. An eccentric lady named 'Camp Meg' lived here in the early 19th century. She dressed as a man and rode a white horse named 'Skewball.' She was skilled in the care and cure of sick animals and her help was often sought by local farmers. On arriving next to a metal gate, cross the stile next to it into the field which has spectacular views in all directions. Continue across this high ground before descending right onto the track that runs between tree-lined enclosures used by Camp Wood Farm. Leave the woodland through the gate to the

GOREBRIDGE: *WALK 7*

The path below Crichton Colliegate Church

parking area beside the farm and continue to the road.

9. Turn right and almost immediately left onto the entrance road for Camp Wood Farm, passing alongside animal paddocks where Highland cattle and goats can be seen. The track ends at a gate through which you pass, to begin your descent down fields where Blinkbonny, an open cast mine, operated until the end of the 1990s.

At the end of this descent, join the road next to a communication tower, turn left and look out for a path opposite that takes you into trees. Cross with care onto this path before quickly turning left to follow it to the edge of a housing estate. Continue downhill past Stobhill School to Burnside Road before crossing to the path that runs across the park to the road below. Cross and continue on the pavement left for Hunter Square then downhill to return to the station.

Vogrie House

Vogrie House is a baronial mansion designed by the renowned architect Andrew Heighton and built-in 1875 on the site of an earlier house belonging to the Dewar family. The house and estate were sold in 1928 to the Royal Hospital for Mental and Nervous Disorders and it became an exclusive residential nursing home. During the Cold War, the house was used as a communications centre and then as a police headquarters. Midlothian Council took over ownership of the house and 2000 acres of Country Park in 1975.

Crichton Church

INTERSTATION *WALK 1*

I1 THREE BRIDGES

If your desire is for a walk full of interest and contrast, then this one is for you. This flat route takes you between Shawfair and Eskbank stations into the area's recent and ancient history. It includes abandoned collieries, old towers and churches a plenty, with connections to royalty and the foremost Scottish architect of the 18th century.

1. Leave Shawfair Station car park along the entrance road where the site of the old Monktonhall Colliery is in front of you. Turn right and follow the pavement as it swings right at a junction and head past housing on your left to where a large hedge appears. Follow this left onto a single-track road to a metal barrier next to a house entrance. Continue onto a

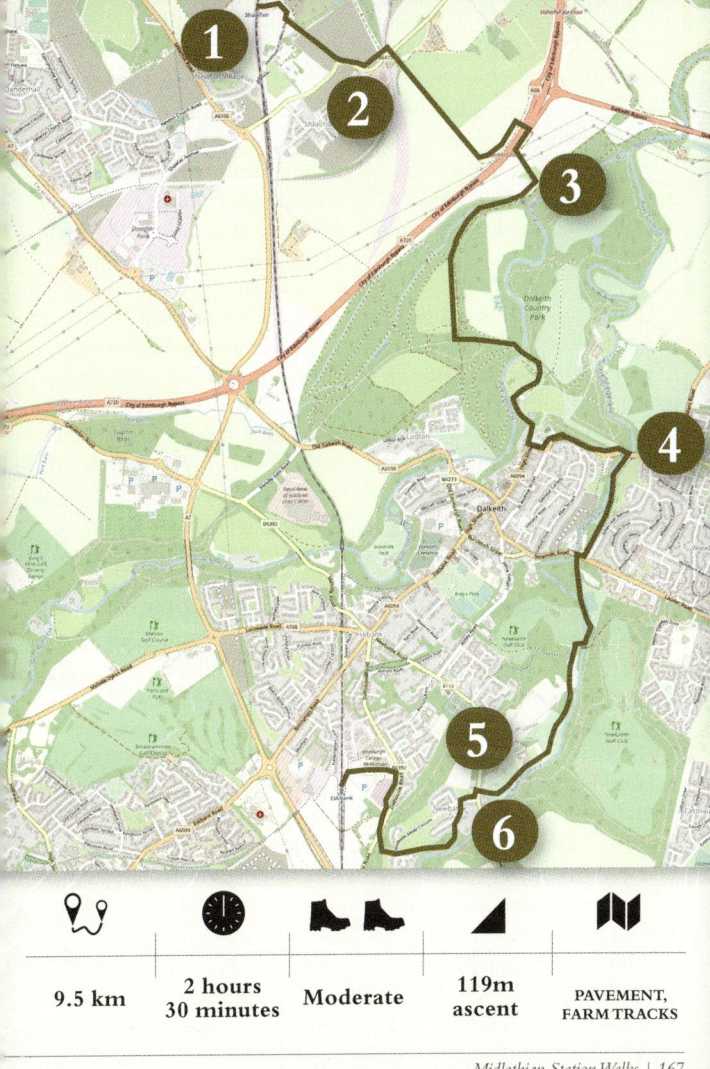

INTERSTATION *WALK 1*

narrow path that runs between rows of hawthorn bushes to the roadside. Turn left and stay on the pavement as it crosses a road junction and head towards Millerhill.

2. Continue ahead over a bridge and just beyond cross with care to join a roadway that descends to a farm track. Follow this track between fields before swinging left, parallel to the City Bypass. Cross the stile and take the underpass into a large field and stay right on the wide track before turning left across fields. Here you can see the remains of Old Newton Kirk and some old gravestones. Clay pigeon shooting takes place in this field at times so take care.

3. Head beyond this to the boundary wall of Dalkeith Country Park, turn right and follow the edge of the field to a gap in the wall about 50m ahead. Drop into the park and turn right on the narrow path and follow it until you meet the estate road, then turn left. Follow the road over Montagu Bridge, a gift to Lady Elizabeth Montagu to celebrate her marriage to the 3rd Duke of Buccleuch, then turn right past the front of Dalkeith Palace. Follow the road past St Mary's Episcopal Church, built in 1843 as a chapel for Dalkeith Palace to leave the Country Park entrance on a cobbled roadway to the main road. Turn left and follow the pavement as it edges the wall of the estate. Cross the road at a set of lights and turn left to reach the footbridge over the river.

4. Cross then turn right into the park and follow the path up a slope into a housing estate where you keep right on the pavement. On meeting the main road turn

Old Newton Kirk
Newton Church was built in 1742 to replace a much older church on the same site. All that remains today is the tower and some gravestones that are still visible today with the rest of the graves under the ploughed field.

The old road that runs through the Monktonhall site

right then almost immediately left at a crossing point to follow a track into Waterfall Park. Continue ahead bearing right to Maiden Bridge, a narrow medieval structure which was once the crossing point over the River South Esk for the ancient Salters Road built by the local monks. Cross then turn left to follow the track close to the river and enter the grounds of Newbattle Abbey College. It is worth spending time admiring the gardens and the two magnificent sundials dating back to 1635.

Monktonhall Colliery
Monktonhall means 'the hall of the farm of the monks', the name deriving from monks at the nearby Newbattle Abbey who was the first to start mining coal in the area during the 16th century. At one time over 1000 miners worked more than 900m below where you are now walking. Imagine what the place would have looked like then with the skyline dominated by the distinctive twin winding towers and the clanking of trains taking the black gold to the nearby power stations.

INTERSTATION *WALK 1*

The bridge to the ice house

Continue past the college and take the footbridge across the river to the icehouse. This was built in the 17th century and filled with ice in winter to store meat and other perishables. Turn right and follow the track through Lord Ancrums Wood to the minor road then take a right to cross the old Newbattle Bridge to the main road. The original bridge dates back in part to the 16th century but was substantially rebuilt by the Victorians. Unusually the downstream refuge is pointed while the upstream side is semi-circular. Head to the main road close to an impressive row of cottages lined with cypress trees.

5. Cross the road with care and within 50m turn left onto the narrow roadway past housing into

woodland. The path meets the banks of the River South Esk where you keep right along the river. Just after negotiating the banking of an old river crossing, continue to a metal railing protecting a storm drain.

6. Turn right here onto the grassland that runs between housing before crossing the road to the bank of trees before you. Find the path in the corner close to a burn and head up the banking into the woodland. Within 500m there is an opening in the wall, cross the road with care and turn right to the entrance road for Eskbank Station past Edinburgh College

Maiden Bridge
This is a medieval bridge over the River South Esk that was built for the monks at the nearby Newbattle Abbey as it was on the approach to the abbey from anybody coming from Soutra into Lothian.

INTERSTATION *WALK 2*

12 BIRDS OF PREY

A short immersive walk that takes in the new and the very old. From modern solar farms and industrial relics to long-established woodland and an ancient castle with its own mews!

1. Leave Eskbank Station and head past Edinburgh College and Dalkeith Solar Meadow, Scotland's first solar farm. On meeting the main road turn right and within a few hundred metres cross to enter woodland through a wall entrance, with a fingerpost for Eskbank. Turn right and follow the path as it drops through trees to the side of a burn with a housing estate beyond. Follow the fence line, cross the road and continue to

INTERSTATION *WALK 2*

Wild Roses

the trees before you.

2. On reaching a metal railing above the River South Esk, bear right and follow a broad track through a woodland of oak and yew trees. The lack of ground plants here is due to the density of the yew tree canopy where little grows underneath, only the occasional whitebeam or ash where the sun penetrates. The path turns right up a bank to the side of a field where you turn left to follow the path to the roadside. Cross the road with great care and continue under the Victorian built Newbattle Viaduct, which now carries the Borders Railway. Keep to the left-hand side of the road as no pavement here.

3. After passing a cottage take the path left into woodland signposted for Dalhousie Bridge. The sound of falling water can be heard through trees on your left, a short diversion allows you to view a large river weir. Further on pass a large boundary wall to Grove House and join a wide track that takes you close to the main road.

4. Before reaching it turn left and head down the roadway into the grounds of Dalhousie Castle Hotel. Built in the 13th century its guests have included Mary, Queen of Scots, Queen Victoria and Sir Walter Scott. Head past the falconry on your left where birds of prey can be viewed, or a viewing can be organised.

Follow the edge of the grass area with splendid views of Dalhousie Castle and as the path drops to the side of a road turn left to cross a small bridge. As the bridge ends take an immediate left onto a narrow path and head up the slope under a covering of trees to a large metal gate. Take the

Falconry
Falconry remains an important part of Arab culture with cave paintings suggesting prehistoric origins. In its traditional form it was used for hunting small animals in the wild but now is used to scare nuisance birds like pigeons and seagulls.

INTERSTATION *WALK 2*

The Sun Inn

Dalkeith Solar Meadow
Dalkeith Solar Meadow was developed by Edinburgh College and designed and installed by SSE Energy Solutions. It was Scotland's first solar farm, opened in 2013, and covers 5 acres generating around 560,000 kilowatt hours of energy (0.6MW) annually. It is used as an outdoor classroom for engineering students and provides an opportunity to study biodiversity around solar installations.

exit by the gate post and turn left to cross this busy road before turning right on the pavement.

5. After a few hundred metres turn left into Butlerfield Industrial Estate and follow the pavement to a metal barrier into a housing estate. Keep right and continue past two side roads to where the housing ends. Turn right down the slope into an area of grassland and follow the footpath under lampposts to the far corner. Head up to the roadside on a winding footpath, turn right and immediately right down the steps to Newtongrange Station.

The lamposts at the National Mining Museum

Yew Trees
The yew is a native tree of the UK and can live for more than 1500 years and is symbolic of everlasting life, rebirth, and immortality. It is associated with places of burial and a feature of many churchyards possibly to stop farmers from grazing their cattle there. The wood of yew was used to make the English longbows in Medieval times. Everything except the red flesh of the berries is poisonous.

INTERSTATION *WALK 3*

I3 — A SLOE WALK THROUGH TIME

A pleasant undemanding walk between two old mining communities. Views of the Pentland Hills open up as you head towards the beautiful Gore Glen woodland before descending past the many fine buildings on Gorebridges Victorian Main Street.

1. From Newtongrange Station take the steps close to the platform to the roadside, turn left, cross the rail bridge then left again and follow the winding footpath as it drops towards a housing estate. Stay right on the footpath under streetlights to the main road through the estate.

2. Keep left and stay on the pavement crossing two road

INTERSTATION *WALK 3*

junctions to a bend in the road then turn left on the clear path (avoid the path directly ahead). Beyond a utility box is Butlerfield Industrial Estate, cross the road with care and follow the pavement right to reach the main road, cross to the other side and keep right.

Looking east on Povert Road

3. Beyond Lothian Cat Rescue, turn left onto the path that drops away from the roadside. This is the oddly named Povert Road which is bordered by Blackthorn bushes that produce a purplish fruit called sloes. There are good views of the Pentland Hills and on the skyline to your left the distinctive winding gear of Lady Victoria Colliery. The path takes a sharp left before you exit onto a single-track road through a gate.

4. Turn right downhill under a narrow bridge to a parking area for Gore Glen Woodland Park. Head into woodland keep left at a marker and follow the Gore Water upstream on a good track. Alder is a very common tree species here, once a key ingredient in gunpowder production. Continue along this wide track as it swings right past a small pond before bearing left under Shanks Bridge. Just beyond take steps up the steep bank and continue ahead to the footbridge over the railway.

Alder
Alder is native to the UK and thrives in cool damp areas like woodland and streams. A mature tree can live for 60 years and grow to a height of 60m. The seeds are a source of food for siskins and goldfinch while the roots can provide a home for otters. A green dye made from the leaves was used to dye the clothes of Robin Hood and fairies. Alder makes good charcoal, an ingredient in gunpowder, and is the preferred wood to make clogs. It is only durable if kept wet and was used in the construction of boats and sluice gates as well as the piles that much of Venice is built on.

INTERSTATION *WALK 3*

Catkins

5. Turn right on the other side to join the footpath and where this ends keep left into scrubland and follow the path as it swings right to a gate into a housing estate. Stay ahead then bear left then right to leave the estate on the footpath that passes close to what little remains of the 16th century Newbyres Castle. Continue past Newbyres Nursery to the main road, turn right and cross to the pavement on the other side and downhill past the Victorian buildings of Main Street to Gorebridge Station.

Povert Road
The oddly named Povert Road dates back to the 17th century and is derived from the nearby Butlerfield which at one time was called Polvert Maynes 'the steading on the stream'.

Dippers
Dippers are a common sight on the Gore Water. Their name comes from their habit of constantly bobbing and dipping as they search the river for food. Also known as water ouzel they are short and stout in appearance and are also characterised by the ability to dive and swim underwater. They trap a thin film of small bubbles on the surface of the plumage to protect themselves when submerged.

INDEX

A HISTORY OF MIDLOTHIAN 14-19
Arniston House *13,127,131,132,133,137*
Borthwick Castle *15,119,154,155,157*
Borthwick Church *114,118,119,154,157*
Butlerfield Industrial Estate *113,177,180*
Camp Wood *110,146,149,150,161,162*
Catcune Castle *118,136,154*
Catcune Mill *115,120,136*
Crichton Castle *156,157,158*
Crichton Church *160,164*
Dalhousie Castle *15,92,95,96,175*
Dalkeith *9,18,19,37,46*
Dalkeith Palace *15,70,80,168*
Dean Tavern *91,103,105*
ESKBANK SECTION 36-87
Eskbank Station *10,37,38,166,171,172*
Gallows Hill *121*
GOREBRIDGE SECTION 114-163
Gorebridge Station *10,140,182*
Gore Glen *126,137,139*
Gore Water *9,114,126,130,137,183*
Hawthorndean Castle *19,44,47*
Hewnan Bank *45,47*
Hunters Square *140,146,149,162*
INTERSTATION WALKS 166-183
Lady Victoria Colliery *17,91,105,169*
Lasswade *19,48*
Maiden Bridge *50,53,58,169,171*
Masterton Wood *8,110*
Melville Castle Hotel *68,71*

Monktonhall *17,23,166*

Montagu Bridge *66,91*

National Mining Museum Scotland *13,17,106*

Newbattle Abbey *15,17,54,55,58,62,63*

Newbattle Viaduct 18,83,65,84,85,97,105

Newbyres Castle *137,142.143*

NEWTONGRANGE SECTION *90-113*

Newtongrange Station *10,177,178,182*

Newlandrig *161*

Old Newton Kirk *168*

Pentland Hills *9,24,37,64,94,105,113,144,148,178*

Polton *47*

Povert Road *92,94,113,180,181,182*

River North Esk *9,19,41,48,77,79,86*

River South Esk *9,54,63,65,77,82,86,97,115,139,171,174*

Roslin Glen *38,42,44*

Rosslyn Castle *41,44*

Rosslyn Chapel *15,17,49*

Shanks Bridge *27,130,139,181*

SHAWFAIR SECTION *22-33*

Shawfair Station *10,166*

Smeaton Bridge *79,80*

Stobmills Gunpowder site *115,123,130*

St Nicholas Buccleuch Church *37,68,81*

The Sun Inn *65,85,86,97,176*

Temple Village *131,137*

USEFUL INFORMATION *10-13*

Vorgie Country Park *13*

Woolmet *28*

A NEW PLATFORM

DRUMLIN WALKS hope you've enjoyed exploring Midlothian but the adventure doesn't stop here. We also have another book – **Border Station Walks**, based on a similar format, giving you the option to contiue to explore the very best of the entire Borders Railway!

FOR ADVENTURES

VISIT OUR ONLINE SHOP
AND SEE THE FULL RANGE...

www.drumlinwalks.co.uk